YOU ARE NOT AT WAR
HEALTHY CO-PARENTING WITH THE ABSENCE OF TOXICITY

———

Jvion Jones

With Chya Barrett

BOOKS BY JVION

You Are Not At War: *Healthy Co-Parenting With the Absence of Toxicity*

Write This Down *| Journal*
(lined notebook)

When You Are Old Enough to Understand: *My Legacy Left Behind*
(Keepsake guided journal)

Extracting Peace Out of Pain: *Life is About Perspective*

Before Eighteen: *The Missing Conversations in Our Communities for Our Young People*

Write This Down *| Planner*
(12-month yearly planner)

Sever The Middleman: *How to Start a Clothing Brand & Produce Quality Apparel from Home*

All books can be purchased at the link below or by scanning the QR code.

www.JvionVision.com

DEDICATION

*This book is dedicated to my son, **Ahmari Jones**.*

You are #MyReason.

I am grateful because of you.

Everything that I write is for you.

You are my legacy.

I love you!

You Are Not At War:
Healthy Co-Parenting with The Absence of Toxicity
Copyright © 2023 by Jvion Jones

Printed in the United States of America

Author: Jvion Jones
Contributing Author: Chya Barrett
Cover design: Jvion Jones

ISBN: 978-1-7363743-8-2

Published by: Ahvision Publishing

YOU ARE NOT AT WAR

HEALTHY CO-PARENTING WITH THE ABSENCE OF TOXICITY

TABLE OF CONTENTS

YOU ARE NOT AT WAR

TABLE OF CONTENTS

TABLE OF CONTENTS

TABLE OF CONTENTS

www.JvionVision.com

Instagram / FB @JvionVision

YOU ARE NOT AT WAR

ACKNOWLEDGEMENTS

Chya, I thank you for being willing to share your perspective and taking part in this book with me. You definitely enhanced it. You are appreciated!

If you've read any of my books, you would know I'm big on including quotes. I'm also big on getting contributing thoughts from people I know to enhance the conversation. I do this because I'm fortunate to know some exceptional individuals with profound wisdom to share with my readers. This book is no exception. I approached my friend, Chya, and asked if she would be willing to share her thoughts related to the topics in the book—just a few quotes that I could incorporate into specific chapters. She agreed and promptly provided a contribution for one of the chapters. What she sent was so impactful that I decided to take it a step further and asked if she wanted to contribute throughout the entire book and be my co-author. She agreed.

At the end of most of the chapters, you will find her remarkable contributions under the title
"A Mother's Perspective"

ACKNOWLEDGEMENTS

To the mother of my son, *Tracey*.

Thank you for being the mother and co-parent that you are. It means a lot that we can show a healthy example of what co-parenting looks like, given our toxic history. Although our son is only seven years old, and we have many more years left to co-parent, I'm hopeful that the next eleven years will look similar to the previous four (fingers crossed). You have been a good partner. You are appreciated!

"When engaging in co-parenting, you are faced with two options: fostering a peaceful co-parenting dynamic or cultivating a toxic environment. Each choice carries its own set of consequences, as is true for any decision. It's crucial to bear in mind that your children are watching and influenced by the choices you make. Opting for a peaceful co-parenting approach not only benefits your own well-being but also sets a positive example for your children, demonstrating the foundations of a healthy relationship."

Tracey Harris

YOU ARE NOT AT WAR

Author's Note

You Are Not At War | Before the war begins; before the household is split apart; before the father goes his way and the mother goes her way; before the children only see both parents in each other's presence during exchanges; before the fight over custody and visitation; before someone finds love elsewhere, there is always that opportunity to hold on to what you have and keep your family intact under one roof before it's too late.—*Jvion Jones*

Co-Author's Note

You Are Not At War | In this book, you will find many powerful gems and even vulnerabilities that I wouldn't have shared with anyone if Jvion had not provided me with a genuine, safe space to do so. Although my thoughts and emotions are valid, I had to learn a mature way to navigate through chaos. Being able to express aspects of my journey with co-parenting has brought a great deal of healing in other areas for me. Recognizing that my "family" may not fit the ideal mold, I hold the ability to nurture a foundation that is uniquely mine. This deserves to be highlighted in a manner that reveals the effort invested, surpassing mere words on paper.—*Chya Barrett*

17

YOU ARE NOT AT WAR
HEALTHY CO-PARENTING WITH THE ABSENCE OF TOXICITY

INTRODUCTION
Causation

War is conflict, fighting, division, disunity, and hostility. War is hatred, bad blood, vengeance, and unnecessary. War doesn't have to involve weaponry or military forces. When two parents who are no longer in a relationship with one another argue every time they speak, that's war. When two parents look for the slightest infractions in the other to pick a fight or prolong a pre-existing issue, that's war. When two parents fight over custody for no reason other than to make the other person suffer, that's war. When two parents refuse to speak to one another unless it involves the children (that's childish, first of all), it's also war.

"You Are Not At War" is about healthy co-parenting with the absence of toxicity. It speaks to the men and women who, at one point, had something special together, whether it was short-term or long-term, one night or one decade, that out of that relationship gave birth to a child who is now being raised in separate households or one. *"You Are Not At War"* is about progression in the wake of separation. It's about more than just tolerating one another for the sake of the children. *"You Are Not At War"* is about family. It's about having a healthier relationship with your co-parent. This book is a message to parents, especially Black parents, that even in separation, you can still be a family.

THE WAR

According to the percentages, nearly 50% of all marriages will end in divorce or separation. 60% involve couples aged 25-39. The average age of individuals who will experience their first divorce is 30. I got married in 2012 at the age of 25. We had one child together, Ahmari Jones, in 2016. We separated and divorced in 2018 when we were 31. Given the divorce rate of individuals in my age range, my biggest concern regarding marriage was never the possibility of divorce but the perceived ramifications of what came after it—war. That was always my thought.

The separation between two individuals who share a child rarely transitions smoothly once they are no longer in a romantic relationship. In many cases, the two parents struggle to coexist, whether the child was conceived within a marriage or out of wedlock. Co-parenting often becomes chaotic or non-existent altogether, with one parent—often the father—absent from the picture. The end of a relationship often signifies the end of a family.

The deeper the emotional investment between the two individuals, the higher the level of animosity and contempt that tends to surface. What makes this situation even more heartbreaking is that it becomes worse when children are caught in the middle. In instances where two unmarried individuals, who were together for only a short period and have no children together, decide to part ways, they can usually do so amicably, with minimal drama beyond the typical heated arguments that typically precede a breakup. Unfortunately, when children are part of the equation and intense emotions are intertwined in a long-overdue separation, it often results in a mixture of drama and conflict within that relationship.

I didn't want a co-parenting relationship with my child's mother where we were constantly at war and just tolerated one another. Due to ingrained biases, I feared not being able to have the same access to my son that I once had when I was married to his mother. I had no intention of being the father who would or could only see his son on the weekends or whenever the mother or courts would allow it. I didn't want to have a son whose mother I hated and whose father she hated. I didn't want to be at war; I wanted to be at peace. I still wanted to remain a family.

THE NUMBERS

It should be evident that fathers have a harder time gaining custody of their children than mothers after a split. We don't even need to refer to official surveys or online graphs; we can observe this in our daily lives. We can look at our own families, friends, neighbors, and coworkers and understand the disparity that exists when it comes to primary physical custody. As of 2018, nearly 80% of custodial parents were mothers. The question I ask myself, and one for which we may never have a definitive answer, is why?

Is it because 80% of fathers don't want the responsibility of being their child's primary caregiver or having more involvement than just visitation? Do they not want to be involved in their children's lives at all? Is it because the system consistently favors mothers 80% of the time? Is the court system biased against men? Are women deliberately keeping children away from fathers out of spite? Have historical patterns contributed to how we approach our parenting roles today? Who or what should we blame? How do we assign responsibility for where the fault lies? My answer: We shouldn't attempt to.

There's one common factor in many failed relationships—pointing fingers from one person to another. Every question from the previous paragraph leads to an answer that will never be agreed upon by all parties involved. Each answer to these questions only leads to endless arguments. Blame is directed outwards instead of individuals recognizing the facts and holding themselves accountable.

"There is nothing better I can do for you
than to make a better me.
There is nothing better you can do for me
than to make a better you."
Phree Tha Truth, Poet

When I heard those words from Phree Tha Truth speaking about co-parenting, I knew immediately that I would be including that quote in this book. It's all about introspection. So, for a moment, let's forget about the numbers, statistics, rates, surveys, graphs, and any other information that tries to divide and blame external factors. I want all of us to hold up a mirror, not just peek through a window. I've learned that for there to be peace and civility in any relationship, especially in co-parenting there are three behaviors that, when embraced by both partners, lead to progress: Acknowledgment, Self-Awareness, and Self-Accountability.

Acknowledgment: Did the expansion of the welfare system in the 1960s significantly harm the lower class, particularly within Black communities, by incentivizing Black mothers with cash welfare if there were no fathers in the household? YES. Before the welfare expansion, from 1890 to the 1950s, did Black women have a higher marriage rate than white women? YES. Did some government programs discourage marriage, creating a divide between families that still lingers today? YES. Does the system seem biased against fathers in most cases? YES.

Now, are there men who are neglectful fathers and do nothing for their children? YES. Are there women who get pregnant solely for child support without intending to involve the father in the child's life? YES. Are there men who think that providing financial support is enough and that spending time with the child isn't necessary? YES. Are there women who do everything in their power to keep the father away from their children? YES. Are there fathers who give up too easily and see no point in fighting for their children? YES. And since I brought it up, should men even have to fight? NO.

Here's my point: The numbers are not always relevant. Phrases like '80% of fathers...this' and '65% of mothers...that' do little to solve the issues in front of us. Debating custody rates from 1963 has no direct influence on whether or not I choose to be an involved father today. I control that, not some percentage. A survey compiled from 10,000 parents in 1993 should not dictate the quality of the relationship between my son's mother and me In 2023. We determine that, not some survey. The only concern is what exists in our present situation, what we can control, and how we can improve. That brings us to self-awareness.

Self-Awareness: Author Debbie Ford defines self-awareness as "the ability to take an honest look at your life without attaching it to being right or wrong, good or bad." What often conflicts with self-awareness is a person's suppressed understanding that their behavior or the reality they're struggling to become self-aware of is wrong or bad. This denial often leads to unfairly pointing fingers at someone or something outside of self. When we become self-aware of our inadequacies, we can take the next step toward correcting them. That brings us to self-accountability.

Self-Accountability: Self-accountability is defined as "an obligation or willingness to accept responsibility or to account for one's actions." Typically, in a relationship, there are two people (excluding my polygamous folks, of course). Those two people share the responsibility of co-parenting. You have complete control over one of those individuals—you. The other, not so much. While there can be an influence, complete control is rarely the case.

It would be nice if I were a deadbeat father and my son's mother, at the click of a button, could take me from never wanting to see my son to being fully invested in his life daily. It would be nice if my son's mother, out of spite, kept my son away from me, and at the click of a button, I could transform her into this peaceful person who would prefer that we raise our child together jointly. Unfortunately, the tech world has yet to invent such a device. So, for now, that leaves us with self-accountability—the "willingness to accept responsibility or to account for one's actions."

Take an honest look at your parenting, co-parenting, and behaviors. Become self-aware and self-accountable, and focus on improving yourself first. To both men and women reading this book, I'm addressing you. What can you do to bring your family together? I understand that circumstances vary, and you may not be the primary source of the problem. You may be on the receiving end of a broken system, an absent parent, a challenging individual, or a horrible human being. You may read this book and think to yourself, referring to your child's other parent, "They need to be reading this book, not me!" You can't control someone else's actions or changes in their life. However, you can control everything within your control.

"When we are no longer able to change a situation, we are challenged to change ourselves."
Viktor Frankl, Psychiatrist

THE REALITY

Here's the reality—Not all wars come to an end. Some fathers may never consistently come around. Some fathers may not come around at all. Some mothers may be spiteful throughout their child's entire childhood. Some mothers may always attempt to alienate their children from their fathers. Some people only invite drama into their lives and relish it. It may continue until the child is eighteen or take longer than one would like it to stop. As much as I hate to say it, some women choose the wrong man to have a baby with; some men choose the wrong woman to impregnate. Some people are just terrible human beings. Unfortunately, some people will never change—at least not within 18 years.

25

Some people are just flawed, as we all are, but they want to change. They may just need a little support. Some people are a bit damaged, but a better version of themselves is buffering inside of them. Some people just need to hear a specific thing at a specific time that will change their outlook on how they view parenthood and the mother or father of their child(ren).

SELF-accountability! I emphasize this word because of its importance when delving into the pages of this book. To be clear, my objective is not to initiate a debate or argument about the subject matter of this book. There is already enough of that on social media when it comes to relationships. My aim is for co-parents to read each chapter, identify the areas in which they can improve, and become better co-parents to the mother or father of their child. I want us to engage in healthy conversations, not debates, surrounding co-parenting. I hope this book can help bring families back together or bring them together for the first time.

CHAPTER ONE

After It Breaks

"If we don't end war, war will end us."
HG Wells, Writer

YOU ARE NOT AT WAR

CHAPTER 1
After It Breaks

Many different reasons can lead to two people parting ways in a relationship. It could be infidelity, abuse, financial problems, incompatibility, or growing apart, to name a few. The reasons for separated households may differ, but the one commonality that many of us share is having to have a continued relationship with the other person because of a child we share. The issues that often arise in that scenario reflect the problems that existed in the broken phase of the relationship—when the foundation became so weak it could not be repaired.

How a relationship ends often influences how we treat and feel about one another moving forward. When a couple without children exits that broken phase and goes their separate ways, they typically don't have to see or speak to each other again. So, if there was any lingering resentment from what may have transpired during the most challenging times of that relationship, it's highly likely that the source of that resentment would not be present in the aftermath. Because of that, the one who felt hurt wouldn't be triggered to release an outpouring of anger toward that other person. Unfortunately, the same cannot be said when children are involved. We have to see that person.

The same toxic energy we exit the relationship with becomes the same toxic energy we will carry into the co-parenting phase. If we spent the final year fighting and cursing each other out, that most likely will not cease the moment we are no longer together.

That hate and toxicity will continue, cloud our thinking, and ultimately affect the child. We live in a world where society has normalized us disliking our child's parent unless we are still together. Drama is expected, and in many instances, it's even encouraged. Because of that, there's more of an inclination to instigate a problem than to diffuse one.

When we enter any situation with a false and biased preconception that 'this is the way it is,' we tend to settle for and accept things more easily. No individual should be expected to have conflicts with their "baby mama" or "baby daddy" solely based on these titles. As strange as it may sound, this issue is prevalent. I believe that part of the problem lies in the terminology we use to identify one another.

"BABY MAMA"

'Tracey' — 'Ahmari's mom' — 'Ahmari's mother' — 'My son's mom' — 'My son's mother' — 'My Co-Parent.' Those are six different ways I can refer to the mother of my child (make that seven). Ahmari's mother, Tracey, and every woman who has given birth to a child have a name. Ahmari's father, myself, and every man who has contributed to bringing a child into this world have a name. I don't use the term "baby mama," and I don't see myself as someone's "baby daddy."

"[Baby Mama] indicates a strained relationship or a person so insignificant that we need a less-than-dignified expression to sum up the individual and our relation to them."
Joel Leon, Writer

I couldn't have said it better myself. There has always been a negative connotation surrounding the terms. In its origin, it is a demeaning reference used to describe a mother whose relationship with the father of her child was primarily sexual and not serious. It stamps an 'insignificant' label on every woman who was never married to the father of her children. The same ideology applies to every father who did not marry the mother of his children. We are more than a stereotypical label.

In our community, when the terms are often used, the way it's interpreted is: "That's just the chick that had my baby" or "That's just the dude that knocked me up." 'Baby mama' and 'baby daddy' can emanate a dark cloud over the parent's connection, importance, responsibility, and respect. A child born out of wedlock should not devalue the mother, father, or their relation to their child. Whether we realize it or not, I feel the usage of these terms plays a role in how we perceive one another. Ultimately, that perception can alter how we treat someone based on the titles we give them.

The words we use matter; terms have meanings; the labels and titles we place on one another have power. I believe in treating everyone equally no matter the title, but we all know the weight one word can carry and its impact on those who use it. Think about 'Vice-President' or 'Associate,' 'Manager' or 'Representative.' Now, let's think about 'Mother' or 'Baby Mama,' 'Father' or 'Baby Daddy.' Which one sounds more significant—"That's her son's father" or "That's her baby daddy?" I see my son's mother as someone who didn't just assist me with having a baby. Our importance in our son's life is equal, and how I refer to her supports that.

"Those terms (baby mama/baby daddy) reduce the importance of the parental role as it implies a lack of emotional connection between the parents, which can hinder effective co-parenting and communication."

"Throw some respect on their titles.
It is truly an honor to be a parent."
Chya Barrett

COLLATERAL DAMAGE

Like many relationships and marriages that would eventually end, Tracey and I had our share of fighting and anger that we expressed to one another during our marriage. We were, what I like to call, at war at one point—a war that continued into our co-parenting phase. We only spoke if it involved our son, Ahmari. There was never any small talk or conversations where Ahmari wasn't the topic. We didn't even say "hi" or "bye" to one another. My mind frame was simple, "If it doesn't concern my son, don't say a word to me."

After we separated in 2018, I moved out. It would take close to one year until the courts finalized the divorce. During that time, we decided on a parenting plan that would be fair to both of us—50/50. But there was still a lot of toxic energy between us. We avoided one another as much as we could. Our relationship was so broken that when we would meet to hand off Ahmari to the other, we did it at fire and police stations. It was unnecessary and necessary at the same time. We couldn't stand each other, and it showed. But no matter how damaged our relationship was, neither of us allowed Ahmari to suffer. He was never collateral damage.

If you had asked me in 2018 how I felt about Tracey, I would have had more negative things to say than positive ones. Let's just say I'm glad I didn't write any books from 2018 through 2019. I didn't like her much as a person. She wasn't always the nicest partner and could be spiteful at times, admittedly so. But I never questioned her dedication as a mother to our son or her respect for me as his father. Over time, that spitefulness that she once displayed began to fade. Her feelings towards me never intersected with my relationship with my son.

Over the years, I've spoken to many fathers and mothers who are no longer with their child's parent. I've heard from both sides every drama flooded and war story imaginable. I've been transparent in my truth and have attempted to give hope to those in rough situations by talking about where Tracey and I once were and where we are now. But it wasn't until recently that I realized that the cards I was dealt weren't as bad of a hand as I previously made it out to be. I think about what a lot of men are currently going through or have gone through with their child's mother, and I gain a deeper appreciation for Tracey.

With everything that Tracey and I have been through, I have never had to fight for custody of our son. There has never been a day where she has tried to keep me from spending time with Ahmari. To hurt me, she has never used Ahmari to do so. When we divorced, she didn't think 'child support' over 'present father.' When she may have resented me, she didn't instill that same energy into our son. Parent alienation, sadly, is one of the most common responses in these situations. I never had to deal with that. There are a lot of good men out here who cannot say the same, and that bothers me.

YEAR ONE

Our storylines may differ. The path I've taken to being a father of a child to whom mother I am no longer with may not be the same as yours. You may have never gotten married; your children may be older; you may be a father who barely knows the mother of your child; you may be a mother who barely knows the father of your child. You may have endured so much pain from your child's parent that it would seem foolish at the idea that the two of you could coexist as a family. But no matter what the differences are, I assume that if you're reading this book, a healthy co-parenting relationship isn't completely off the table.

"The first year of co-parenting is the toughest because you ain't even thinking about the kid."
Donnell Rawlings, Comedian

I heard that during an interview Donnell Rawlings gave on the popular radio show, *The Breakfast Club.* Essentially, he was saying that after a breakup, many people become so fixated on what the other person did to them that they pay little attention to what's actually best for the children. Their sole focus becomes resenting their child's parent. When they look at that individual, all they can see is the person they've been fighting with over the years, the person who made them angry, the person they were fed up with, the person who didn't offer support when needed, the person who wasn't emotionally available, the person who cheated on them, the person who may have abused them—the person who hurt them. They also just see the person they are no longer with, and for that reason, it's war.

34

Reaching a point where you have a healthy co-parenting relationship may take some time, perhaps as long as the year Donnell Rawlings mentioned or even longer. Now, one of the central themes of this book is self-accountability. With that in mind, if you're the reason why your relationship with your child's other parent remains contentious and at war, I hope this book will inspire a change of heart by the end of Chapter 6. If you're not the reason why your relationship continues to be chaotic, remember these four words—space, time, patience, and calmness.

Space and time are for them; patience and calmness are for you. Space and time are what they may need, while patience and calmness are what you'll need to have. You may find yourself in a situation where every time there's communication, it's accompanied by an argument or attitude. Everything about how you're being treated indicates that you're seen as the enemy. There may come a time when silence is the best response.

When they're clearly not ready to be cordial, your first step should be to remain calm. If they send negative energy, don't send it back. Avoid prolonging arguments in an attempt to make a point; you won't win, especially when dealing with someone responding emotionally. Remember, they may have strong negative feelings towards you right now. Allow space, time, calmness, and patience to eliminate any toxicity that exists in their mind towards you. Don't react emotionally, either. Keep your personal business off social media, and never slander the name of the person you share a child with. Keep in mind, that's your child's mother or father. Lastly, be patient. Change, growth, or forgiveness will not happen overnight.

A MOTHER'S PERSPECTIVE:
"He's JUST My Baby Daddy"

"I've been blessed to have four terrific children, each with their own uniqueness. My oldest son is 14 years old. Additionally, I have a set of twins, a boy and a girl, who are 11. Initially, the relationship didn't work out with their father, and we chose separate paths while still prioritizing our children's well-being. Yearsss later, (huge gap)...I had another child, a beautiful baby boy who is now 1 year old. Despite the absence of a romantic relationship with his father, we continue to prioritize and maintain a strong co-parenting partnership.

Strong co-parenting relationship and all, I was most definitely one of those females who would address my children's fathers as, "Oh, he's JUST my baby daddy." I could not understand the big fuss and negative context that "baby mama" and "baby daddy" held as I looked at it as a form of acknowledgment to my co-parents. Once I became open to understanding that those words were not true forms of endearment and carried less value and emotion, I changed my viewpoint. I wanted to show respect and use inclusive language when referring to my co-parent as either the father of my child or by calling them by their government name. I mean, they were given those names for a reason.

When you show respect by how you choose to acknowledge your co-parent, it shows the importance of the parental relationship and the responsibilities that contribute to a healthier co-parenting dynamic and create more positive interactions. Words hold power. The last thing you want to do is use a term that comes off as demeaning or disrespectful."

— **Chya Barrett**

CHAPTER TWO

Co-Parents, NOT Competitors

"Nobody wins when the family feuds."
Jay-Z, Business Mogul

CHAPTER 2
Co-parents, NOT Competitors

"**A** state of mental or emotional strain or tension resulting from adverse or very demanding circumstances." That is the definition of stress. Everyone has different stress triggers. There's a long list of things we can all go through mentally, emotionally, and physically that can put us in a dark place. It could be minor or major, and what you may consider "minor" may be "major" to someone else. Life stressors affect us all in different ways.

So, what are some of these causes of stress? We encounter four primary categories: financial, work-related, health-related, and relationships. Within each of these categories, the stressors become even more specific. The question isn't whether or not we'll encounter life's stresses during our lifetime; we all know that's automatic. The more important question is how we deal with them when that time does come. What steps do we take to alleviate and ultimately remove a particular stressor from our lives? That question will be important when we think about stress stemming specifically from a co-parenting relationship. First, I want to explore these different causes.

Financially-Related Stress: This typically arises from financial constraints or dissatisfaction with one's current financial situation. It may be due to not earning enough to sustain a desired standard of living or a specific lifestyle.

Work-Related Stress: This type of stress is associated with job or career dissatisfaction. It can stem from various factors such as the nature of the work, working hours, treatment at the workplace, salary, working conditions, and more.

Health-Related Stress: This category encompasses stress caused by chronic illnesses, emotional challenges, dissatisfaction with one's body weight, and even losing a loved one.

Relationship-Related Stress: This stress arises when one is unhappy in a relationship or with their partner, regardless of the underlying reasons.

When you're not earning the desired income, a solution to the stress-inducing problem is to increase your income. When you're unhappy with your job, finding another job is a solution to the source of your stress. If you're dissatisfied with your weight, a solution to the stressor is to either lose or gain weight until you reach your desired level. When you're unhappy in your relationship, a solution is to work towards its improvement or consider ending it altogether.

There is always a solution to every problem. However, before we can approach a solution, we must decide to work toward one. As I mentioned, a person unhappy in a relationship (without children) can easily end that relationship and alleviate themselves of the stress that comes with it if they decide to. They can, and they usually do. They make the decision and take action to make their situation better. They detach because they can.

40

Your wife or husband doesn't always have to be your wife or husband. Your girlfriend or boyfriend doesn't always have to be your girlfriend or boyfriend. Your bae doesn't always have to be your bae. Your friend doesn't always have to be your friend. But your child's parent will always be your child's parent. There is no option to break up. You will always be connected because of the child or children you share. Even in separation, you are still tied together. Therefore, if there's a type of relationship where we should invest an immense amount of energy to ensure it remains healthy, it's the one with the person we share children with. Unfortunately, we often fall short in this regard. At best, we tolerate the situation and accept it as the way things are supposed to be.

That's why we'll fight to better our relationship with the person we're in love with but not the child's parent that we're not. We believe "it's supposed to be drama." Civility doesn't have to leave just because the love is no longer present. No one should accept that a co-parenting relationship is predetermined to be stressful and chaotic. Personally, the most stress I have ever endured was directly connected to the mother of my son during the time we were in our broken phase. That's not an indictment on her, by the way. It has more to do with the situation than the individual. Once we checked out emotionally and concluded that we did not see a future with each other, our treatment of each other reflected it. Thankfully, we got ourselves out of that mental warzone we were in. I just want the same for everyone else

"Co-parenting. It's not a competition between two homes. It's a collaboration of parents doing what is best for the kids."

Heather Hetchler, Author

41

SAME TEAM

Let's use a basketball analogy: In the 2014-2015 NBA season, Steph Curry won the season MVP. Not only was he the best player on his team that year, but he was arguably the best player in the league. He's the greatest shooter this world has ever seen, by the way. That same season, the Golden State Warriors would defeat Lebron James and the Cleveland Cavaliers in the NBA finals to become the 2015 NBA champions. If I were to ask most basketball fans, before the start of the finals, who they thought would win the finals MVP in a Warriors victory, most would say Steph Curry. Surprisingly, Andre Iguodala won the finals MVP that year, deservingly so. I don't want to take anything from his performance.

The following season, the Cavaliers would defeat the Warriors in the finals. The next season, the Warriors signed Kevin Durant to a two-year contract. Curry, who had averaged 30 points per game (ppg) the year before Durant's arrival, dropped to 25 ppg the year he played with Durant. Durant, who had averaged 28 ppg with the Oklahoma City Thunder, dropped to 25 ppg while playing with Curry and the Warriors. With Durant joining the Warriors, they would go on to win the next two championships, and Durant would be crowned the finals MVP of both.

Here's the point: Sacrifices were made; points per game decreased; attention was shifted, and the accolades didn't always go to the player everyone expected, but everyone on that team got what they all played for—an NBA championship. Those players were on the same team and shared the same goal—to bring home an NBA title at the end of the season.

The Warriors didn't win any of those titles because of one player. It was a collective team effort. Yes, Andre Iguodala won the finals MVP in 2015, but Steph Curry averaged 26 ppg. Yes, Kevin Durant won the finals MVP in 2017, averaging 35 ppg, but Steph Curry, again, also contributed 26 ppg in those finals. Yes, Durant won the finals MVP in 2018, but Curry averaged 27 ppg. Everyone who played added something that contributed to seeing a 'W' in the win column, including the players I didn't name. Winning is a team effort. Durant's 35 ppg means nothing if Curry only averages 12 points, and they lose the finals. The plan is for each player to do their part and for the team to succeed.

Team success will always supersede individual accolades. I don't have to always get on the court and drop 60 points. Sometimes, I can dish out 12 assists and grab 8 rebounds. I don't have to be "MVP." I just have to be on the court and do my part. It's the win that's most important, not my pride. Think really hard about that in terms of co-parenting. In every co-parenting relationship, the parents are the players; the families are the teams; raising children to become happy and good people as young adults is the championship. It's the ultimate goal. That is what we should all want. I want my son, Ahmari, to reach his eighteenth birthday and know that he was raised by two loving parents who put his best interest before their own.

NEGOTIATION

"Negotiation is a dialogue between two or more people or parties to reach the desired outcome regarding one or more issues of conflict. It is an interaction between entities who aspire to agree on matters of mutual interest. The agreement can be beneficial for all or some of the parties involved."

That sounds like every relationship to me. There's a constant reoccurrence of negotiating and being in the position of having to compromise when co-parenting. Most joint decisions between parents are made by negotiating one way or another. It could be a short exchange of dialogue, a heated argument, or days of continuous back and forth. It could be one parent saying, "This is what we should do," and the other saying, "I agree," or, "I guess." It could also be, "This is what we are going to do," and the other parent not having much say in the matter.

I'll give an example of a time when Tracey and I failed to reach an agreement about something, and we had to make a mutual compromise. Ahmari was close to three years old when Tracey and I separated. For a few months, we were still living together. He attended a daycare Monday through Friday that was perfect for both of us, given our living situation at that time—all being under the same roof. However, once I prepared to move out, our work schedules and new living arrangements would no longer be conducive to the daycare he was attending. So, we had a conflict—I couldn't take him to daycare in the mornings.

The daycare opened its doors at 7:30 a.m. I began work at 6:00 a.m., while Tracey didn't start work until 8:00 a.m., so she could still take him to daycare. However, for me, that wasn't possible. I did have other options, though, and although not all were favorable, there was one that made the most sense—changing the daycare to one that opened earlier. So, I found one that opened as early as 5:00 a.m. But, for whatever reason, she ultimately didn't want to make the switch. What now? We've agreed to 50/50 joint custody and exhausted all options, including the most logical one.

The only other option I could think of was to put Ahmari in both daycares. She drops off at the daycare of her choice on Monday/Wednesday/Friday, and I pick up; I drop off at the daycare of my choice at 5:00 a.m. on Tuesday/Thursday, and she picks up. It wasn't the result I wanted for numerous reasons, but it was a compromise she agreed to and worked out.

The objective is to come to a mutual decision. It's hard to do that when two people are not aligned in certain areas. It's even more complicated when one parent can't stand the other or both parents can't stand each other. That's when the negotiations can quickly turn into only wanting to settle on a decision where one parent gets the upper hand on the other. It goes from being impartial and fair to illogical and one-sided. The attitude behind every conversation where a decision has to be made is, "I don't care what we decide. I just don't want them to get what they want."

Cooperation over competition is key. Co-parents are not competitors of each other. Whether for selfish reasons or just having a different opinion, doing what's best for the child first should be prioritized. Next to that is what's fair and best for both parents, not just one. What do we all need to do as a team that makes everyone happy and gets us closer to that ultimate goal—for our children to become happy and good people as young adults—to reach their eighteenth birthday and know that they were raised by two loving parents that put their best interest before their own.

A MOTHER'S PERSPECTIVE:
Logic Vs. Emotions

"When I think about self-accountability, it brings forth the dynamic of logic vs. emotions. I remember being deep in my pettiness of emotions about things I wanted to control, and Jvion asked me, how would you feel if the shoe were on the other foot? How would you like your children's fathers to acknowledge, treat, or show they respect you? I realized then that it was less about them and more about how it would affect my children. I had two choices—I could stay bitter in my feelings about what I do not like, OR I could accept the reality for what it is and move forward in maturity. I would like to think the love towards our creations would be enough for us to desire a healthy co-parenting relationship.

The overall goal should be to provide and maintain a stable and nurturing environment for our children. By keeping that goal at the forefront, I am certain it will contribute to a positive co-parenting relationship and ensure your child will thrive. Managing your emotions and holding yourself accountable while interacting with your co-parent will help avoid confrontations, heated arguments, or involving your child in disagreements. Self-accountability is not saying your feelings are invalid; it is keeping the idea of a composed and respectful demeanor that will bring growth to the relationship. It is almost as if you have to stay ready and willing to check yourself in any area that needs improvement and make necessary adjustments that assess your own actions and behavior as a co-parent. Let that "shoulda, coulda, woulda" shit die and think about the gain your children will receive if you move with more logic and less emotion." — **Chya Barrett**

CHAPTER THREE

Language

"Most people do not listen with the intent to understand; they listen with the intent to reply."

Stephen R. Covey, Author

YOU ARE NOT AT WAR

CHAPTER 3
Language

In the introduction, I clarified that finger-pointing was never the answer. I also made it clear that self-accountability was vital in co-parenting relationships. So, we have to address the elephant in the room. Here's the reality: The system's power over the child is often taken from the father by the mother and then handed over to the system, intentionally or unintentionally. To use a basketball analogy, they get an assist. The pecking order of custodial parenthood appears to be the mother at #1, the system at #2, and the father at #3. The order in which the father is listed depends on the mercy or control of the mother. It is also determined by what the father is willing to accept.

So that begs the question, how do we change that? We first start by changing our thinking. By changing how we think, the words we use change, and so does our behavior as a result. As people who are products of our experiences and what we see daily in society, we have these ingrained biases that largely contribute to our relationship with our child's parent. Both men and women view themselves a certain way because of historical patterns related to parenting roles.

Historically, the mothers are the presumed primary caretakers, and the father's presence in the child's life is at the mother's discretion. Mothers are often viewed as "single mothers," while fathers are just there for child support. Co-parenting should never feel transactional. That isn't the reality for all, but it is the reality for many.

"SINGLE PARENT"

An expecting unwed mother may find out she's pregnant and immediately go into the mind frame of, "OMG, I'm about to become a single mother." That same thinking can continue after the child is born—"I am a single mother." That way of thinking implicitly removes the father from the picture. If this were the case and the mother was a single mother whose child had an absent father, I can understand the designation. However, I can't understand when terms like that are used while both parents are active in the children's lives. It creates an invisible line (one we don't always notice) of division and exclusion. The same goes when the father is the custodial parent. It further detaches away from the family aspect.

Wikipedia defines a 'single parent' as "a person who has a child or children but does not have a spouse or live-in partner to assist in the upbringing or support of the child." Google defines it as "a person bringing up a child or children without a partner." Both definitions imply that only one parent is involved in the child's life. A way of putting it that has an even more negative undertone is that it implies that one parent is absent from their child's life. We usually categorize them as "deadbeats."

I was recently having a conversation with my oldest brother, Jason. He expressed how proud he was of me, his "Lil brother." He started to list accomplishments and qualities in me he admired. Jason would note that I've always been a good kid, I've never been to prison, I'm an author, a great father, and I do great work in the community with the youth. He also commended me on how I handled myself following my brain cancer diagnosis and surgery.

50

All of which I agreed with and thanked him for acknowledging, but there was one thing he called me during that praising that I had to correct him on—a *"Single Father."*

Although it's not the ideal way of raising a child, single parents are often put in a special box of parental admiration for doing the one thing alone that is hard to do with two people. To call someone a good parent and then remind them that they are doing it by themselves is a compliment and a way to tell them, "You are strong and resilient." It's like giving more credit to the NBA player who had less help to win an NBA championship than the player who had two other all-stars on his team. That was Jason's intention when he emphasized that I was not only a good father but doing it as a "single" one. Where I disagreed, respectfully, is that I am not a "single father."

"...It (single mother / Single father) can be perceived as a bit misleading or confusing to others. It traditionally implies that a parent is solely responsible for the child's upbringing without any involvement from the other parent..."
Chya Barrett

Tracey has always been in Ahmari's life. Now, if you followed me on social media years ago, you may have had the same assumption my brother had. I went from sharing public posts about my wife and photos of the three of us as a family to no longer posting Tracey at all. Whenever I'd post, it would only be photos of Ahmari and myself or Ahmari by himself. So, I can understand people assuming that I am a single father if they rarely, or never, see any sighting of the mother.

That said, here's what confuses me with the word "single" and the way in which it's often used when describing a parent: It's that even when two parents are involved but co-parent in separate households and the child may spend more time with one parent than they do with the other, that parent that is the primary caretaker is often seen as a "single parent." The only prerequisite to receiving this "single parent" label is by not being in a relationship with the child's parent. Whenever someone calls me a single father or asks me if I am one, my response is always the same. Jokingly but seriously, I respond: *"Single Man—Yes. | Single Father—No."*

There's a difference between a *single parent* and *a single person*, a *single mother* and a *single woman*, and a *single father* and a *single man*. Tracey and I divorcing doesn't automatically transfer her into the "single mother" category. My involvement determines that. Although we live separately, we both contribute to Ahmari's upbringing physically and financially. I am present daily in his life, and so is she. Neither one of us is doing this alone. My son isn't being raised in a "single-parent household." He just has two households with a parent in each.

I acknowledge that we operate as two distinct households, with each of us assuming full responsibility in our respective homes. I understand that it looks much different parenting separately than it does raising children together under one roof. I also recognize that there are single parents who face a complete lack of involvement from the other parent, or their involvement is so inconsistent that it only makes sense to describe themselves as "single." I comprehend this reality. However, in my case, I simply identify as a father. There is no need for the "single" prefix—just a father who co-parents.

DISTORTED PERCEPTION

Why does this even matter? The first issue is the distorted perception it gives. When I hear dialogue from or about a woman, for instance, and in that dialogue, it's mentioned that she's a single mother, my first thoughts are of the father's involvement. Naturally, questions and/or assumptions will enter the mind. The questions are valid—"What's up with the father? Is the dad present?" Both are questions that, given the scenario, I understand. However, the assumptions one might have could encourage the wrong perception about someone or a group of people. "Another deadbeat father not taking care of his kids," one might assume. When people hear "single mother," they often think "absent father." Not to say it's intentional, but I feel It's discrediting to the men who take care of their fatherly duties to identify as or label someone else as that when you know the father is present.

Let's look at the divorce between actress Tia Mowry and her estranged husband, actor Cory Hardrict. They were married for fourteen years and had two children, and the moment they separated, Tia Mowry became a "single mom." In interviews and articles, that was the narrative being circulated. I searched Google, and the headlines I saw on almost every website were about how she's dealing with life as a "newly single mom." My question is, sarcastically, did Cory up and move to Cuba or something and abandon all his daddy duties that quick? Based on his Instagram feed, I don't think so. And to be clear, this is no indictment on Tia Mowry or any woman that uses the term to describe themselves or others when they know the father is present. It's only to highlight the power that two words can have when used in a particular context. In my eyes, Tia Mowry was not a single mother—she was now a mother who is a single woman.

NORMALIZATION

The second issue is normalization. Because single motherhood is so widespread, we're used to it. In a way, we've become desensitized to situations where we find out that a woman is a single mother. Unfortunately, the single-parent household is a prevalent living arrangement. After decades of the same visual, it's become somewhat of an expectation for many people to see that outcome. I know I'm not surprised when I meet a woman whose child's father doesn't play an equal role in their child's life. I'm not surprised when I speak to a man whose biggest concern is how often he gets to see his children. So, how does our being desensitized to this outcome negatively impact the relationship and dynamic between the mother and father?

To answer that, we have to discuss not just the prevalence of single mothers but how easy it is for many women to accept being one. Remember, accountability. First, I want to go back to when I spoke of single parents often being put in a special box of parental admiration for doing the one thing by themselves that is hard to do with two people—caring for a child. I compared it to an NBA player winning a championship with no other all-stars on his team outside of himself. For those who know basketball, Damian Lillard will get more respect and credit for winning a title with the Portland Trail Blazers than Kevin Durant did when he won two with the Golden State Warriors.

If we look at all the NBA champions throughout the years, we'll quickly find that not many teams have won with only one all-star player on their roster. It's usually two or more. I could make an argument for a couple of teams, but in the end, "not many." They are exceptions to the rule. There aren't a lot of examples of the opposite.

Consequently, what does that do to the minds of most NBA players, experts who cover the sport, and fans like myself who enjoy watching? It acts as evidence that for a team to win, there can't just be ONE superstar player doing all the work. Look at the teams with only ONE superstar, then look at the teams with multiple star players, and it becomes pretty easy to pick which teams will be going home early in the playoffs. The players know they need someone else, and those on the outside (commentators, fans) feel it even more. We hear it all the time: Jordan never won until he had Pippen; LeBron didn't win until he joined up with Wade and Bosh. Kobe wouldn't have won without Shaq and Pau Gasol.

On the other hand, we've seen countless examples of single mothers who were able to lead their children into adulthood by themselves or with very little help. That becomes a badge of honor. There are examples all around us of successful, happy, and productive men and women in society today who are products of a single parent, particularly a single mother. That outcome for a parent is equivalent to winning an NBA championship. This raises the question once more: How can it impact the relationship and dynamic between the mother and father?

The significant distinction between the NBA analogy and raising a child alone is that many women may feel they have sufficient evidence to support the idea that, "I can do this by myself. I don't need a man." Likewise, some men may think, "She can do this by herself; she doesn't need me." We live in a world where mothers are often expected to be the primary caregivers with custody of the child, while fathers are expected to provide child support. That alone isn't co-parenting—that's a transaction.

If a mother doesn't feel that she needs the father to help raise their child, that can lead to many different outcomes. That can encourage the mother not to ask for help; that can encourage the mother not to require the presence of the father; that can even encourage the mother to push the father away. And we all know what often further encourages that last one—child support. If we don't feel we need something, then chances are we won't work hard at obtaining or holding on to it. We have to get into the mindset of needing one another. That thought process is the foundation of building a strong co-parenting partnership.

If I am about to carry an object, the size and weight of that object will determine whether I could or should transport that object by myself. The heavier and larger the object, the more difficult it becomes to lift. In fact, an object can be so heavy or so large that it is impossible for one person to carry it alone. Some objects require one person. Some objects require or recommend multiple. I need help carrying a 250 lb. refrigerator. I need help carrying an 84-inch-long sofa. Sure, I can find a way to get a 76x80-inch mattress and bedframe up a flight of stairs, but it would be much easier on me if I had someone else present to help me.

Metaphorically speaking, a child is a billion times heavier and larger than any object we will ever come across. I don't care if we have the strength to lift (raise) an object (child) by ourselves. Unless we have no other option due to some extenuating circumstances, every child should be lifted by two or more people. Every child should be raised by both the mother and father. Not just monetarily but physically. The more we want and need one another, the more that outcome is a possibility.

A MOTHER'S PERSPECTIVE:
Word Choice

"The context of "single mother," "single father," and "mother who is single," and "father who is single" are often used interchangeably, but there can be a subtle difference in the emphasis. When you highlight and focus on the term "single mother or father," it is a person who is raising their child or children without a partner or spouse. The term directly focuses on a parent's status and role in providing care and support for the children on their own. Sometimes, when we use the term "single mother or father" when the other parent is involved but not in a romantic relationship, it can be perceived as a bit misleading or confusing to others. It traditionally implies that a parent is solely responsible for the child's upbringing without any involvement from the other parent.

Even if you opt for a different wording, such as "mother who is single" or "father who is single," it still implies the individual's personal status regarding their marital situation or the absence of a partner. The term "single" in this context always places a strong emphasis on the relationship status rather than their role as a parent. With anything, it is important to remember that our word choice and intent hold power. Language and labels can carry certain connotations and assumptions, and people might interpret them differently based on their own experiences, perspectives, and cultures. Some may view "single mother or father" as negative, while others understand it in a broader sense to include situations where both parents are still involved. Ultimately, the choice of terminology is up to you.

If you feel that "single mother or father" accurately captures your experience and the level of involvement the other co-parent has, you can certainly use it. However, if you want to emphasize the co-parenting arrangement, you might opt for language that reflects the shared responsibilities. There is a growing understanding that families come in various forms, and the language we use to describe them should reflect that diversity. The key is to use language that accurately represents your situation while minimizing potential misunderstandings." — **Chya Barrett**

CHAPTER FOUR

You Are Family

"The Black family of the future will foster our liberation, enhance our self-esteem, and shape our ideas and goals."

Dorothy Height, Activist

CHAPTER 4
You Are Family

You are family. Having this understanding is the most important aspect of co-parenting. I feel it's the most important because It's a truth that I believe many co-parents don't embrace. I don't even think it's a thought in most cases. Depending on a person's relationship with their co-parent, some people may have read the first sentence in this chapter and said to themselves, "hell nah, you trippin!" Some men may genuinely hate the mother of their child, and for good reason. Some women may genuinely want to trip the father of their child down a flight of steps, and for good reason. The hesitancy to consider your co-parent 'family' could be many personal reasons. There can also be a few obvious explanations. I looked up the definition of family from multiple sources, and here's what I got:

DEFINITION OF FAMILY

Definition #1: "A family is a group of persons who come from the same ancestor." (Merriam-webster)

Definition #2: "A group of two or more persons related by birth, marriage, or adoption." (hrsa.gov)

Definition #3: "A group of one or more parents and their children living together as a unit." (Google)

Those definitions should come as no surprise to anyone. We know the meaning of family from merely existing. But I wanted to share those because there are some contradictions between those "definitions" and my assertion that co-parents are also family. We all have a mother and father (parents). Many of us have brothers, sisters, aunts, uncles, cousins, etc. We call them family. But "co-parent" is never mentioned in that same group. According to the definitions, these are the key identifiers of what a family is:

1. Having an ancestor in common
2. Related through birth/blood
3. Related through adoption
4. Related through marriage
5. Parents w/children living together

One of the prerequisites for being a family is having a shared ancestor in common. An ancestor is someone related by blood that came *before* you. I would argue that what also makes two people family is shared offspring (someone related by blood that is here because of the two of you). Do Tracey (my co-parent) and I have an ancestor in common? No. Are we related through birth or blood? No, I hope not. That would be weird. Are we married? Not anymore. Do we have a child together and all living under the same roof? Child—Yes; living together—No. If we take the literal meaning of family, by definition, Tracey and I are not. My (our) son is my family; her (our) son is her family, but we (Tracey and myself) are not family. We were family at a particular point, but that ended the moment we were no longer married. I couldn't disagree more with that notion.

You are all family. The mother and father don't need a marriage certificate, share the same last name, or have the same blood running through their veins to determine that. Those aren't the only qualifications for what a family is. The one qualification that many of us appear not to include is a shared child. When we look at our co-parents and start to see them as family, we begin to treat them as such. We respond differently to them than we would to someone that we just see as our "baby mama" or baby daddy." Stop treating your co-parent like your co-worker. It doesn't mean we forgive them for whatever pain they've caused us, buy them gifts on every birthday, or invite them as a guest to our wedding. It doesn't mean that conflict will no longer arise because of a change in perspective. What it does lead to, however, is the significance of that person in your and your child's life especially, is given a much more powerful meaning to it.

All of us have family members we don't speak to. The vast majority of us have friends that we have more of a connection with than we do with our own blood family. Many of us have family members that we don't get along with. Some of us may even have family members whom we would use the word "hate" to describe the way we feel about them. That's nothing new. How we feel about someone does not change the fact that they are our family. I say all that for those who may find it difficult to look at their co-parent, the mother or father of their child, and see them as family because of how their relationship and interactions have playod out with one another throughout the years. Always remember what ties the two of you together. Married, living together, romantically involved or not, that other person that went half on a baby with you is your family.

FAMILY DAYS

Disclaimer: This ain't for errbody! Consult with your significant other, if you have one, prior to doing this. Ahmari was almost 3-years-old when Tracey and I divorced. He's 7-years-old now. His age has always been the most important factor in our co-parenting schedule, as I feel it should be for anyone. Co-parenting a 16-year-old looks completely different than co-parenting a 6-year-old. When Tracey and I first divorced, there was no sense of togetherness. We both adopted the "Don't speak to me unless it involves my kid" attitude. The only time Ahmari was in the presence of both of us was during exchanges for no more than 5 minutes.

As Tracey and I became more cordial (no longer in the, "Don't speak to me unless it involves my kid" phase), I would always notice the difference in how he acted when all three of us were together versus just two. His energy would already be 100, but with Mom and Dad in close proximity, now it's 120. The smile would be brighter. The laughs would be louder. The goofy would be goofier. And that's to this day, by the way. That's what I've noticed over the years with him. To put it simply, he's happier when he's with the both of us. So, how are we able to give him that family experience if we are both no longer together? His mother and I don't have to be together, together. The answer is "Family Days."

We've always done things together as a family. We try to make it a point to have a family day when we can. It's not often because of our schedules, but we are intentional about giving Ahmari that experience. We understand the impact that it has on him at such a young age, to be able to spend quality time with both his parents. Again, his age is an important piece as to why we have family days.

I don't see us still doing this when he's 16 or 17 years old other than attending sporting events and his graduation, but at ages 5, 6, 7, 8, 9, etc.—it's essential.

Our family days are simple. We may go out to eat, to the park, to the movies, to an arcade, or to a museum. Earlier this year, we all went indoor skydiving as a family. That was hilarious, by the way. Apparently, this little dude thought he was in a swimming pool by the way his arms and legs were flailing! That was a great experience for him that he wouldn't have been able to share with his parents if we always tried to keep one another at a distance. We also spend Christmas and Halloween together, even if it's only for a short period. Your family day doesn't have to be elaborate; it can be as simple as going for a walk or taking a moment to talk during exchanges. This is far better than having a purely transactional relationship where it's just, "Here you go. I'm out."

Now, I understand that this whole "family day" thing may never be a possibility for many people. There's a man somewhere reading this right now (could be you), who read all that and said to themselves, "My lady would kill me. You trippin." There's a woman somewhere reading this right now (could be you), who read all that and said to themselves, "My man will kill me. You trippin." For those who are in relationships, I understand. Just bringing up the idea of this concept to your significant other may cause friction. But for those who are single, or those who have an understanding partner, figure out what the best compromise is that works for everyone. Here's one idea: Who says your significant other can't also be there?

TESTED

In life, there are ups and downs, peaks and valleys, and peace and war. As Rocky Balboa would say—*"The world ain't always sunshine and rainbows."* We have to learn to take the bad with the good. That also applies to co-parenting. Problematic situations, minor or major, will present themselves. It's how we react in those situations that determines whether it stays in the category of a potential problem that never materializes or grows into a nuisance.

"I feel like I'm being tested."
Chya Barrett

We will be tested. Implementing everything that I talk about in this book will not make your co-parenting relationship perfect. You will still have disagreements. They will still say or do things that will get on your nerves. If we could change one thing about our co-parent, I'm sure we can all find something. For example, I can't stand when Tracey sends me an "smh" text or that damn palm-over-the-face emoji in response to certain things I text her. I also don't like it when she "dislikes" those texts—Stupid iPhone feature. I just think it's disrespectful. Am I trippin'? Is it just me? And yeah, I know that was three things, but I'm just venting here.

My point is—minor or major, you will be tested. What annoyed you about that person when the two of you were together is most likely the behavior they still have. And we are not off the hook either. We will also test our co-parent. We also do and say things that trigger a certain response from our co-parents, whether it's called for or not. The question on both parts is, how should we all react?

What should you do when your co-parent, intentionally or unintentionally, makes you upset? What should you do if they insult, demean, and disrespect you? What should you do when you are tested?

First, recognize that you probably know your co-parent in many ways better than they know themselves. You know if they're just saying something intentionally to trigger you. You may know if they're the type to speak before they think and don't really mean what they say. And you may also know if you can "check" them without making matters worse.

Second, what's the best response that will not make matters worse? In other words, if I try to "check" this person, will they say, "You know, you're right. I was wrong." Or will they respond with more nonsense and try to prolong the drama?

Your co-parent may say something you don't like, and you respond in a way they don't like—now the two of you are going back and forth for the next 3 hours or 3 days about nothing. Your entire day or week was ruined because the two of you wanted to "win" the conversation. Not everything deserves a response. Think, how do we resolve this in a peaceful manner, not who can say the most hurtful things about the other? If you know your co-parent is trying to make you upset, don't show them that upset person. if they're the type to speak before they think and don't really mean what they say, just don't respond to their nonsense. Give it time. And don't be on the initiating end of the nonsense, either. To sum this all up, we all have the power to either diffuse a situation or light the spark to it.

A MOTHER'S PERSPECTIVE:
Receiving Truth

"While being tested by the other co-parent causes frustration, typically, some sort of emotion is tied to it. An emotion that is triggered through a preconceived notion stemming from the dynamic in which the relationship was. Co-parents may not trust each other's decisions or actions when they have a strained or adversarial relationship. Testing can be a way to confirm their doubts or concerns about the other parent's intentions or abilities. It can also be a way to assert control or power over the other parent. Sometimes, co-parents who do not like each other may engage in testing as a way to express their frustration, anger, or resentment toward the other parent.

A major key that has helped with my co-parenting partnerships is seeking to know myself. Knowing that I am an overthinking, emotionally sensitive individual, I had to find balance in the root of what my co-parent may want to say, even if it is not delivered effectively.

An example of receiving truth without effective communication: I had a disagreement with my co-parent. Once he realized that I was not going to back down on my thought process, he decided to bring up an old situation unrelated to the current conversation with the intent of provoking a reaction. While I wanted to go ham, I was quickly able to remove emotion and find truth. It was at that moment I learned three valuable lessons through my co-parenting relationships:

1. *Do not take anything personally. In being eager to grow, listening is essential.*

2. *Constructive and respectful testing can be healthy if there is effective communication, cooperation, and mutual respect.*

3. *Sometimes, we are being tested as a form of self-protection. They may want to ensure that they are not being unfairly burdened or manipulated and are seeking a sense of trust without saying it.*

Overall, we all have our quirks of things we do not like about others. It really takes an ideal focus on the child's best interests in order for things to run smoothly." —**Chya Barrett**

YOU ARE NOT AT WAR

CHAPTER FIVE

Fifty-Fifty

"Children spell love... T-I-M-E."
Dr. A. Witham

YOU ARE NOT AT WAR

CHAPTER 5
Fifty-Fifty

Every child has parents with their own factors that weigh into deciding what custody will look like for them. It could be the type of neighborhood both parents live in, the circumstances surrounding either parent, the distance each parent lives from each other, the proximity to the school the child attends, or the age of the children. That last one is especially important. Depending on those factors, following a schedule split directly down the middle may not always be in the child's best interest. If either parent is battling some sort of addiction or mental disposition while trying to raise a child, then maybe joint custody isn't the best choice. If the mother lives ten minutes from school and the father is an hour away, I can understand the father primarily having the child on the weekends. In the end, custody splits will look different for everyone. It is the starting point that matters.

In Chapter 2, I defined the term "negotiation." It is the process by which entities try to reach mutual agreements, with the potential that it could benefit all or some of the involved parties. In the business world, it's common for one party to seek a larger share of the deal, and it's typical for two business partners to engage in negotiations, with Partner A sometimes believing they deserve a more significant percentage than Partner B due to their perceived higher value. Unfair deals and unequal splits are prevalent in business, but in co-parenting, both parents should come to the table and start with a **fifty-fifty** approach. 50/50 should be the default option and starting point.

Before the courts are even involved, so many fathers are content with whatever time the mother gives them with the children. And to not place most of the responsibility on the mothers—a lot of fathers only show up when it's convenient for them to see their children. Being a "weekend daddy" was never a role I would welcome. Being a "summertime daddy" would only make sense to me if Tracey and I lived in separate cities, and she just so happens to live in the one with the better school district. We are both fortunate to have a co-parent that wants the same thing. There was never any pushback from either of us when we discussed custody. We always had the understanding that if we were ever to divorce, "you ain't getting no damn full custody and leaving me with every other weekend. What the hell I look like?" At least, that was how I thought. I can't speak for her, but I'm willing to bet it was something along those lines, just maybe worded differently.

"I want full custody." Whenever parents divorce or separate, three essential matters must be addressed: Custody, decision-making, and child support—who gets the kids, who makes the decisions on their behalf, and who provides financial support. There's another aspect that parents, particularly those going through a divorce, may need to consider: Property division—do we sell the house and split the proceeds, rent it out, or keep it? If we decide to keep it, who keeps it? Only one parent can reside there; it's an all-or-nothing decision. If both parents want the home and do not reach an agreement, that is the only time it makes sense that a parent would have an "I want it all" attitude and fight for 100% ownership of that house. However, that same way of thinking shouldn't also be applied to custody battles. There shouldn't even be a "battle" to begin with.

Before I delve into that, let me say this in case I haven't already (and probably have)—not all parents are fit to parent at any given time. There are many real-life examples where one parent primarily takes care of the children while the other parent only has visitation, and there are logical reasons for this arrangement. Some parents are so toxic or such terrible individuals that they don't even deserve access to their children. I'm just being real. For these parents, I understand a one-sided custody arrangement or even none at all. However, excluding these exceptional cases, the conversation about custody should never begin as "me OR you" but instead as "me AND you."

It confuses me whenever I hear about a famous couple splitting, and details surface that one parent is seeking full custody. The question I always ask myself is, "Why?" What could be the logical reasons behind that thought process? Because there could be. However, the harsh reality is that often there isn't one. Famous couples or not, the reasons are often rooted in spitefulness, selfishness, or the response of a controlling person. A better question that I have is, Why go with **fifty-fifty** joint custody? Why should a 50/50 arrangement (or as close to that as possible, given your unique situation) be the default option?"

DEFAULT OPTION

1. 2 is better than 1
2. Fathers can teach their sons what a mother can't.
3. Mothers can teach their daughters what a father can't.
4. The absence of a parent impacts children.
5. Parents can use a damn break.

Most, if not all, of what I listed may be obvious. I don't even think I need to elaborate on #1. We should already understand basic math: 2 (parents) is better than 1 (parent). What about 2 and 3? Do we all understand the advantage fathers have over mothers when it comes to raising young men? Do we understand the advantage mothers have over fathers when it comes to raising young women? Do we also understand that men can instill certain qualities into their daughters that a woman may find difficult to do? Do we understand that women can instill certain qualities into their sons that a man may find difficult to do?

Let's look at it like this (analogy alert!): A mother and father each have a toolbox. Inside each box is an assortment of tools both have acquired throughout the years. The toolbox's purpose is to teach our children what each tool is used for and how to use them. The ultimate goal is to pass on those tools to our children so that when they encounter a problem where a specific tool is needed, they will have access to it and be able to fix whatever problem they have. Here's the issue—every toolbox is different.

First, no one has every tool inside of their toolbox (and I mean that both figuratively and literally). It's always something missing. Second, there are tools that we've never seen before. Third, there are tools that we know about but have no idea how to use them. We may have tried, but we can't quite figure it out. Fourth, there are tools we can use a little bit, but we don't know how to effectively articulate to someone else the proper way to use them. In short, we, individually, don't know it all or have all the answers. But here's the solution to that problem—Our co-parent.

Our co-parent may have some tools in their toolbox that we don't have. Our co-parent may know how to use some tools that we don't know how to use. We may have many of the same tools, but our co-parent might have better-quality ones. So, what is the point of this analogy? We can't teach our children everything as an individual. The child needs as much of the mother and father as possible. I can guide my son in a way that his mother can't. She can teach our son in a way that I can't. So, who's needed more? That shouldn't be a question, argument, debate, or conversation; both are equally required. Stay in that space and way of thinking. Now, what about 6?

The absence of a parent impacts children: Children are affected in many different ways. The less involvement a parent has in their children's lives, the more it can affect the child in the long term. We've all heard the term "daddy issues," for example. It's amazing what a couple more hours a day, days a week, or months in a year can do for a child's growth, self-esteem, and mind as they become adults. Children need physical presence more than they need direct deposits. I have yet to see a child grow up and ask his or her father, "Where was my child support when I was 10?" It's always, "Where were you?" "Why weren't you there?"

"Money does not equate to time, investment, and energy needed from both parties. Losing my father at a young age was enough for me to know that I would not want that for my children if I could help it."
Chya Barrett

A DAMN BREAK

Let's talk about one more reason why 50/50 (or as close to that as possible, given your unique situation) should be the default option when co-parenting—parents can use a damn break. I'll speak for everyone (and I hope I'm right) when I say we all love our children more than anything in this world—more than life itself. We love spending time with our children. We love the attention we get from our children. We love the sight of our children. We love raising our children. We even love the things that annoy us about our children. And no matter how much they get on our damn nerves at times, there is no better place we'd rather be or better person we'd rather be with than our children.

However, speaking for everyone, we lead busy lives. We may work anywhere between 40-60 hours a week. We may have 2-3 jobs. Many of us are running multiple businesses. Some of us are enrolled in school while working full-time. We have meetings and events we've committed to. We sleep. We commute. All this is secondary to our primary commitment—being a parent. When do we truly have time for ourselves? How can one individual carry the weight on their shoulders of the responsibility of two people without getting weak at some point? I want to paint two different pictures.

Note: This is a scenario that I'm sure is familiar to so many parents (not just mothers). For the sake of the example, I will use mothers as the primary subject, but I recognize that many fathers also find themselves in the challenging situation I'm about to describe.

Scenario: A mother has sole custody of her two young children. She works 5 days a week. Every weekday morning, it's time to go into mommy mode. She wakes the kids, prepares them for school, and then takes them there. She then goes to work, where she'll be in work mode for the next 8 hours. After work, she returns to the school to pick up her kids. When they get home, it's back into mommy mode— homework, playing, dinner, redirecting, yelling, more redirecting, more yelling, cleaning, etc. No help. At some point, the entire house goes to bed, wakes up the following day, and does it all over again. There's no work or school during the weekend, but mommy mode is still activated.

How much stress could be added to her life because she never has time for herself? Eight hours a day at work isn't a break. Eight hours of sleep while the children also sleep isn't a break either. How much easier would it be on her if the father picked the kids up from school on some days? A married couple who lives together share the responsibility of caring for a child. Everyone's situation is different, but we can all agree that, in some way, both parents contribute daily. For a full-time parent doing it alone, it's the complete opposite. As I said before, generally speaking, we all love our children more than anything in this world—more than life itself, but if you are a full-time parent of a young child who says you don't need a break, you're lying! As the youngsters say, "That's cap."

"I had to be honest with myself in knowing I am not one of those, "I can do it by myself, "I don't need any help other than for you to cash me out" type of mothers. I absolutely need and want the help from the person who co-created with me."

Chya Barrett

Here's the alternative to that scenario. For myself and my co-parent, Tracey, we have what's called a parenting plan. A parenting plan simply outlines how separated parents will raise their children. We both have 50/50 custody. There are different parenting time schedules that co-parents subscribe to. What works for us is alternating each night of the weekday and alternating weekends. Here's what our plan looks like on paper:

PARENTING PLAN

Sunday (Mom)
Overnight / takes to school Monday morning.

Monday (Dad)
Picks up from school / takes to school Tuesday morning.

Tuesday (Mom)
Picks up from school / takes to school Wednesday morning.

Wednesday (Dad)
Picks up from school / takes to school Thursday morning.

Thursday (Mom)
Picks up from school / takes to school Friday morning.

Friday (Dad)
Picks up from school

Saturday (Mom / Dad)
Alternate weekends

Ahmari was approaching three years old when Tracey and I divorced and divided our households. His age was a huge factor in the parenting plan we selected. Until then, I had never gone a day without seeing my son. I couldn't picture not seeing him for an extended period. Two days was one day too much. So, there was no way I wanted to go with a week-on and week-off schedule, for instance. With our plan, we're both able to see Ahmari every day, excluding every other weekend when the other has him.

There are many ways to split custody so that one parent doesn't have to bear all the responsibility. On page #133, I've listed seven examples of custody plans. One of the seven is an *alternating week* schedule. One parent will keep the child for one week and then switch with the other. Pretty self-explanatory. A second example from that list is called a 3-4-4-3 schedule. One parent will have the child for 3 days, and then the child will go with the other parent for 4 days. Then it switches—the first parent gets the child for 4 days, and the second gets the child for 3 days.

With any of these schedules, both parents get a fair amount of time with the children. The child can spend a significant amount of time with both parents. No one bears all the responsibility. No one should feel cheated. And here's the icing on the cake—both parents get a damn break. That "break" amounts to time—*time* for that 2nd or 3rd job you may have to work; more *time* for the one job that you currently work; *time* to finish up that college degree you've been working towards; *time* to work on your business; *time* to go on vacation. Most importantly, *time* that will give you the space you need to make sure your mental health is where it needs to be—*time* for SELF.

81

A MOTHER'S PERSPECTIVE: Stop Being Bitter
By Chya Barrett

"Free Game: Stop being bitter & LET THEM KIDS GO WITH THEY DADDIES! "Long story short, I didn't like the father of my baby, and the feeling was mutual. Well, maybe I did like him a little, but I was mainly upset that he chose another woman over me. Nevertheless, we shared a child together. Since I couldn't control his choice, I felt the need to control the co-parenting situation. I imposed certain conditions on our co-parenting arrangement that I knew would bother him. He wanted 50% custody of our son, but I was reluctant to agree. I insisted on every other weekend, and that was final. As time passed, I came to realize that I was doing both myself and our son a disservice by not sharing custody, especially since it takes time to gain a sense of normalcy after giving birth. It took a few instances of my son being away from me to recognize that this situation was a blessing in disguise. Not only did I get time to myself to move without restraints, but it also saved me money since I wasn't solely responsible for his care.

"The more I released control, listened to what his father wanted, and honored his wishes, the easier things became for me. By choosing to move forward with ease, we were able to cultivate a friendship not only between us but also with his wife. This made co-parenting easier in all aspects. I can ask for whatever is needed to care for our child, and I receive it 95% of the time. Instead of using my child-free time to worry about what he's doing, who he's doing it with, and why things are the way they are, I've focused on investing in myself. I have been able to fully grasp that emotional responses in trying to control situations will ultimately hurt and take away from the greater benefits available." — ***Chya Barrett***

CHAPTER SIX

PAPERWORK

"The core of the problem with modern child support laws is that there is too much emphasis on and not enough focus on getting fathers involved in their children's lives."

Cordell & Cordell

YOU ARE NOT AT WAR

CHAPTER 6
Paperwork

We fell in love. We got engaged. We got married. We had one child. We bought a home. We had some problems. We separated. We had more problems. We agreed to divorce. We discussed custody—we agreed on 50/50. We discussed child support—we agreed no one would pay any. We had more problems. I filed papers. We had a big problem. I moved out. We went to court—we disagreed on what to do with our property. Because of that, we couldn't get divorced. Months later, we came to a mutual decision. We went back to court. We finalized the divorce. We continued to co-parent.

That was our pathway into our co-parenting phase in a nutshell. What's noteworthy in all of this is the role that marriage played during the process. Because we were married, we had to sit in front of a judge and establish an agreement concerning custody and child support before we were granted divorce papers. Here's what stood out: My rights as a father were already established. I didn't have to engage in a custody battle for my son or jump through hoops to be a part of his life. My perspective wasn't immediately dismissed the moment I entered the courtroom.

The path to 50/50 had a much clearer view. Because of our marriage, our transition into the co-parenting phase occurred on a more level playing field compared to what it would have been if we weren't married. This isn't to suggest that all or most divorced couples experience easy transitions, but my experience was quite distinct from that of many unmarried fathers who seek custody of their children.

Custody rates look much different for married couples post-separation than for nonmarried individuals with children. Only a mother's rights are automatically established when an unmarried mother has a child. The mother becomes the sole legal authority, and only she has the right to make decisions on behalf of the children. The father has to establish his rights separately through the courts. So, out of the gate, men are at a disadvantage. From the child's birth, an invisible line divides the father and the child. Fathers are rendered irrelevant in many instances. The court system can have more power over the child than the men who went half on bringing them into this world.

There was a time when I disagreed with going through the court system to handle matters that would only involve my child's mother and myself. I figured, why get the courts involved if we agree on everything? Why do I need to have some piece of paper that outlines when I can see my child and how to parent? If we are not in a custody battle, we are in agreement on everything, and we can successfully talk things through like two adults, why do we need a judge? Those were questions I once asked myself—questions that, through observation and comparison, I now have answers to years later, and understand the benefits of it.

I don't know the feeling of wondering when I'll be able to see my son—but I know a lot of fathers who do. I don't have the fear of my son's mother deciding that one day she wants to move across the country, taking our son with her, and there's nothing I can do—but I know fathers whose children live thousands of miles away that they rarely get to see. I've never questioned the rights or power that I have to make decisions on behalf of our son—but there are thousands of fathers who can't say the same.

COURT INVOLVEMENT

That's why I support going through the courts. Tracey and I have a legally binding document that serves as a set of rules that outlines what we can and cannot do, who has our son on this day and that day, who claims him on their taxes during which years—we alternate, and who makes the important decisions—we both do. Everything is equal. And we don't always stick to the plan that's outlined in that document. As a matter of fact, I'm going to ask Tracey if she can pick Ahmari up from school next Wednesday because I have plans. On paper, Wednesdays are my days to pick him up, but we always work together. If she can pick him up, great. If not, no problem. I'll make adjustments and make sure I'm parked outside my son's school on Wednesday at 3:00 p.m. as usual.

There are no legal repercussions on her if she's not able to, or just doesn't want to pick Ahmari up from school on that Wednesday. It's my day, not hers. And I shouldn't even be upset with her if, for whatever reason, she doesn't make the adjustment. Now, if after years of co-parenting, I noticed that I'm the only one making the adjustments, and taking Ahmari for her on the days and weekends that are not mine, and it's never reciprocated, then I'd be irritated as hell. And I'll speak for her when I say that she would, too. Luckily for us, that's not the case. We adjust. Nothing is carved in stone. We swap days, weekends, pick-ups, drop-offs, etc. Sometimes, one will have Ahmari for an extra day and not ask to swap, and other times, we'll swap so we can still have our day. Collaboration is essential. What's also important is not having too high of an expectation of Tracey to always be able to accommodate my request. I understand that it's never an obligation.

On paper, we both have specific days for custody. Having a court-approved parenting time plan helps to ensure fairness and collaboration between us. Not that we needed a court agreement to be fair and collaborative with each other (I know I don't), but it provides added motivation for us not to act like two crazed, spiteful fools. It also keeps us on a level playing field, which I believe is the most crucial aspect. No one has absolute control.

Tracey cannot just up and move from Arizona to New York, taking our son with her, without discussing our custody arrangement in court first. Can either of us move whenever and wherever we please? Yes, but due to our existing custody arrangement, neither of us can just drive or fly off into the sunset with that little boy we created together without entering a courtroom.

LEVEL PLAYING FIELD

On a more local level (I got a little dramatic and nationwide with that last example), neither of us can keep our son from the other without also ending up in a courtroom. I have a legally binding document that states I have my son on specific days. She has that same document that states that she has our son on specific days. If either of us decides that we want to keep him for five weeks straight without consent or communication with the other person, that would be considered a violation of the court order. Now, I am not a family court attorney or expert. I am only speaking from experience, observation, and the research I've done. I don't know 99.9% of how the courts operate. What I do know is that if you want to be on a level playing field with the mother or father of your child, get it on paper.

CHILD SUPPORT

I thought long and hard about which direction I wanted to take this topic because, to be honest, just thinking about it bothers me—and I'm not even on child support. I'm bothered by the insane amount that many of the fathers have to pay to the mother of their children. I'm bothered by the women who would rather receive child support than have an active father in the lives of their children. I'm bothered by the women who don't have their child's father on child support initially, but because they get upset with them one day (for something non-fiscally related), they go to the courts to open up a case for it out of spite. I'm bothered when men who are already taking care of their kids are still subjected to paying child support. And to the person reading this, if you're bothered by something that I haven't mentioned—I'm bothered by that, too.

"Child support should do just that—support children, not the federal government."
Paul Ryan, Politician

Here are my thoughts on child support: If a man refuses to support his children financially, put his ass on child support. If a man refuses to support his children physically and financially, definitely put his ass on child support. Even if the mother makes six figures—if the father chooses not to contribute, put his ass on child support. But if a man is doing what he's supposed to do as a father for his children—he's in their lives, he's helping to pay for the things they need, why should he also be forced to pay an amount (an excessive amount in many cases) in child support?

As I mentioned, I'm not on child support. The way Tracey and I manage our financial responsibilities related to our son is simple: The financial responsibility belongs to the parent whose care our son is in. When he's with me, I'm responsible for keeping a roof over his head. I provide for his needs, including food and clothing for my home. On the other hand, when he's with Tracey, she takes care of these aspects. Additionally, the gaming systems and electronics he uses at each of our homes are also covered by the respective parent. In fact, I just received a bootleg Gameboy in the mail 20 minutes ago that I paid $26.38 for off Amazon.

Now, to clarify something after reviewing the last paragraph. I realize it might come off as a bit non-collaborative, as if we're both saying to each other, "You're on your own." That's not the case, at least not entirely. While we do handle certain expenses independently, we also have shared financial responsibilities. For instance, on the 1st of every month, the fee for Ahmari's afterschool program is due. Expenses like that we typically split. The bottom line is we just try our best to act like adults. Our relationship is not transactional. It's not about money but has everything to do with raising our son.

Here's the beauty of 50/50 joint custody (or as close to that as possible, given your unique situation): Since I have our son 50% of the time, and Tracey has our son 50% of the time, there's no grey area where either of us is crunching numbers trying to calculate how much money we deserve to get from the other in child support. I have everything on my end taken care of, so does she on her end, and we meet in the middle when we need to. Neither of us depends on the other financially.

The moment I go to her and say, "You know what I was thinking—Why don't you keep Ahmari for 6, maybe 7 days out of the week? I'll just pick him up for a few hours during the weekend and take him somewhere fun. I can even keep him overnight for you sometimes if you want. Is that coo?"

If that was our arrangement, and I stopped contributing financially to his upbringing, put my ass on child support! But since we are both doing our part as parents (both physically & financially), keep my ass off child support. I'll do the same.

A MOTHER'S PERSPECTIVE: Control Factor

"My kid's father has always been pretty lenient and flexible about a lot of things. He just wanted to be the one to control his money. Meaning if the kids needed something, he would rather take them to get it, or pay for them to get it. He had an issue with giving me the money directly for something that they needed or wanted. So what I realized is that it was a psychological matter with him. After we split, I filed for child support. Shortly after, we got a court date, but because he wasn't served in a timely manner, he didn't have to show up. Instead of rescheduling another court date, we had a conversation, and he told me that he didn't mind paying child support, but whatever amount they said he'd have to pay, that's all I would be getting from him.

So for me, it was simple. It's like, Okay, I get more by letting him be in control of his money. Even now, to this day, we have certain things that we're technically supposed to go half on that he covers the entire amount for because he still has that leeway. So I just use that same method with my youngest baby's father. I think what helps is that I really don't ask for anything. Rarely do I ask for money. I just go with the flow unless it's something that I desperately need help with. Like with diapers, for example. If our son needs diapers, I just text him and say, "Hey, can you send me diapers?" I don't say, "Hey, can you send me money to get diapers?"

Again, I feel it's a control factor. Men desire a sense of control, authority, and the freedom to make decisions as they see fit. I believe that by allowing them to have this sense of control, I can achieve better outcomes, compared to going to court where that just pisses them off and make them feel less of a man." — **Chya Barrett**

CHAPTER SEVEN

Be The Definition

"Peace cannot be achieved through violence, it can only be attained through understanding."

Ralph Waldo Emerson

YOU ARE NOT AT WAR

CHAPTER 7
Be The Definition

On the front cover of this book, I have several words individually placed inside puzzle pieces. These words represent various qualities and behaviors that, when incorporated into your being and relationships, can lead to a healthier outcome. I want to dissect each of these words, beginning with their meanings, and then establish a connection between these qualities and their positive impact on co-parenting relationships.

Compromise: *An agreement or a settlement of a dispute that is reached by each side making concessions.*

Compromising means being fair and equitable. It entails finding a middle ground and indicates personal growth. It's what we'll need to maintain a peaceful co-parenting relationship with our child's mother or father. To compromise successfully, it helps not to approach a conversation or situation with a desire to be petty.

Reliable: *Consistently good in quality or performance; able to be trusted.*

Be a man or woman of your word. If you say you're going to do something, follow through with it or make an honest effort. Be present, reliable, and trustworthy. Be someone your co-parent can have confidence in and depend on.

Fair: *Without cheating or trying to achieve an unjust advantage.*

Fairness is about reciprocity. This morning, Tracey sent me a text and asked if I could pick up Ahmari from school later today. I responded with a thumbs-up emoji (the brown-colored one, I might add). Since I don't have any important plans at that time, I don't mind picking him up on a day when it's her turn. This action alone could be seen as an example of collaboration. Where it becomes fair is when I ask her to do the same; she has no obligations during that time, and she responds with a brown-colored thumbs-up to indicate her agreement. Since I helped her out, it would only be fair if she reciprocated.

Considerate: *Careful not to cause inconvenience or hurt others.*

To be considerate, it helps first to put yourself in that other person's shoes. Ahmari's school recently had parent-teacher conferences. With both of our busy schedules, it wouldn't be logical or considerate if either of us reserved a time slot for the meeting without first checking the availability of the other. We both want to be present, and we always are. So before I locked in a time slot, I made sure to send her a text asking which day and times worked for her. I was considerate of the fact that she might have had something scheduled at a specific time. Be respectful of your co-parent's time and the things they have going on.

Communication: *The exchange of ideas and thoughts between two or more individuals.*

Communication is key. If either of us is going out of the state with Ahmari, we let the other know. I bet not wake up one morning, scroll Instagram, and see a photo of our child posing in the center of New York Times Square, and the whole time, I thought he was 16 miles away. Communication, not permission. Neither of us necessarily has to ask the other if we can put Ahmari on a plane to go somewhere, but we understand the importance of communicating the intentions to one another. I trust my son's mother to take Ahmari to California to visit his grandmother. She trusted me when I took Ahmari to Las Vegas to meet his great-grandfather for the first time. Communication is all we ask of each other. Communication, not permission.

Communicate, never assume. There's a Jazz festival that I'm going to in a couple of months. The day of this festival is during a weekend that I'm going to have Ahmari. So, what I made sure to do was ask Tracey if she would be able to keep Ahmari during that day. I'm not going to wait until the day before, assuming she has no plans, and surprise her with a text that reads, "Aye. I'm going to this show tomorrow. You think I can drop Ahmari off in the morning?" Here's another example. I have staycations that I go on every 2-3 months. Being the considerate co-parent that I am, I always schedule them during a weekend that Tracey has Ahmari. Now, even though the expectation is for me to be child-free, I still communicate my plans with Tracey so that she knows I won't be available that specific day in case she's looking to make plans that would require that I keep Ahmari for her. Communicate, never assume.

Support: *To give assistance, approval, comfort, or encouragement.*

Tracey is the mother of my son. I want her to be happy, stress-free, safe, and at peace. Why? Because she's the mother of my son. Her mental state affects our child. The same goes for me. So, in whatever ways I can show my support to her, I'll do that. If she's the most important woman in my son's life, then she's also high on my list.

Support isn't always requested, but it's always welcomed. There are times when I'll send Tracey a text and do a mental health check to see how she's doing. And if she's dating someone, please believe I'm keeping an eye out for bruises and marks. Why? Because that's the mother of my son. If she tells me her man cheated on her, that's her business—if she tells me her man put his hands on her, now that's my business. Why? Say it with me: because she's the mother of my son. I care about her, as I should.

Appreciation: *Recognition and enjoyment of the good qualities of someone or something.*

Appreciation is as simple as a text. Not only do I send Tracey messages to check on her, but I also send her texts at random to let her know how much I appreciate her. I let her know how much of a great mother she is. I tell her I'm fortunate to have her as my son's mother. I tell her that I'm proud of her. That goes a long way. When we show our appreciation, trust that it is appreciated. That simple gesture can change the relationship we have with one another for the better. For those who are deserving of it, show it to them.

Forgiveness: *Stop feeling angry or resentful toward someone for (an offense, flaw, or mistake).*

This could have been listed first. Forgiveness is for you. It allows us to move on. If we continue to harbor resentment and anger towards someone, we will continue to be damaged. Forgiveness is healing. It won't change the past, but it can repair it.

Apology: *a regretful acknowledgment of an offense or failure (admitting when you're wrong).*

Conflict often arises when triggering, disrespectful, or demeaning words are spoken. Misunderstandings and misinterpretations can also give birth to conflicts. Have you ever jumped to conclusions, only to discover later that you were wrong? This situation is particularly common in text messages, where we've all encountered a message that we completely misconstrued, leading to an upset response—one that may have offended the message's receiver. Whether we unintentionally offend someone through text, over the phone, or in person, it's essential to apologize when we make a mistake.

If we find ourselves reacting strongly due to a misinterpretation, it's important not to simply carry on as if nothing happened but to offer an apology. This demonstrates accountability. Though this gesture may seem minor, it holds significant value. Not only can it promote healing in the other person, but it can also serve as medicine for your soul. In the words of my big brother, Brother James, "You'll thank me later."

Understanding: *The ability to learn, judge, and make decisions.*

Understanding and comprehension are similar, with a slight difference. Understanding is empathy. Understanding is compassion. Understanding is kindness. Understanding is not entirely agreeing with someone's decision but understanding the why behind it. Understanding is having an open mind.

Love: There are three ways to express.
"I got LUV" — "IN Love" — "I Love"

"I GOT LUV" is a way to show respect. It could also be used for someone we may not know too well, but we know they're good people. "Oh yeah, Charles from 83rd that works at T-Mobile in the mall? Yeah, "I GOT LUV" for him. He looked out for me when I got my phone."

"IN LOVE" is the deepest level. It's what you are while in a relationship. Emotions and feelings are involved in a vastly different way than regular LOVE. Being "IN LOVE" will make you do some crazy things.

"I LOVE" is deep affection. "I LOVE" is care. "I LOVE" usually carries a history and connection between people. "I LOVE" is how we feel about our family. "I LOVE" is what we say to our loved ones, family and friends. "I LOVE" is how I still feel about the mother of my son. "I LOVE" is what we still say to one another. We are family.

Family: *Two or more people related by blood through a shared ancestor or connected together through shared offspring.*

I talk about my personal experiences with my son's mother, Tracey, a lot in this book. The reason is that I want to be an example and proof for those who need it that it's possible to have a non-toxic relationship with a person you once couldn't stand to look at. I understand that there are levels, all situations are unique, and not everyone can or is willing to get to the same place Tracey and I are in. But I hope that it can, at the very least, be improved.

We went from silent exchanges at police and fire stations to meeting at our homes and checking in with one another. Instead of individually splitting the day with Ahmari on his birthday, we now spend that time together as a family. Initially considering alternating holidays each year, we decided to split the day instead. That quickly progressed into spending it together as a family. Every October 31st, the three of us engage in a family activity. On December 25th, I bring gifts to Tracey's house, and we cherish that moment together as a family. My son doesn't have the luxury of growing up with both his parents in the same household, so the least his mother and I can do is offer him a glimpse of that experience as often as possible.

Peace: *Freedom from disturbance; tranquility.*

Peace is priceless. Peace is what we get when we incorporate the definitions of all of these words into our lives. Peace is what we all need.

A MOTHER'S PERSPECTIVE:
The Conversation

"I remember conversing with my oldest children's father about me being pregnant under circumstances that were not ideal. I was super emotional and unsure of how to proceed in a situation that didn't seem promising. My co-parent reminded me that even though this child wasn't his, and he had no legal responsibility, he would offer support in the best way he could. He reassured me that this child would not be treated any differently than his own biological children. When I asked why he was so understanding and welcoming of my situation, he explained that by me knowing I had his support, it would help me stay mentally healthy, and that, in turn, would benefit our children as well.

He shared with me that I was not alone and that we were family. At that moment, I could truly understand the great benefits of keeping the focus on the children as we are a direct reflection and hold access to their mental health and stability. I was reminded that unconditional love and support are needed during times when decisions seem unfavorable. Not only did he keep his word to treat my son as his own, even though his father was very much present, but his blood family followed suit and celebrated him just as his siblings. When you treat your co-parent as family, you create a family-oriented mindset and aid in stability for the child(ren). It welcomes effective communication, which allows cooperation and teamwork. It brings forth positive role modeling, emotional well-being, and smoother transitions because, let's face it, life most definitely be life'n.

Creating a space where your co-parent is looked at as family reduces stress and tensions, which will lead to better mental health and overall happiness. Your child will be able to move between both homes more comfortably, as the environments will be interconnected. You are able to easily create shared memories and experiences that your child will cherish as they grow up. When you choose to recognize your co-parent as part of your extended family, it encourages gratitude for the role they play in your child's life while fostering a positive perspective on your co-parent.

I would even go as far as to say, although you would hope for your children's situations to be different as adults, raising their children in a two-parent household, treating your co-parent as family allows them to see if things do not work out, it does not mean you have to stay in the relationship to be an amazing parent. Ultimately, treating your co-parent as family reflects a commitment to your child's well-being and the desire to provide them with a nurturing and supportive environment. It leads to a healthier and more positive influence on your child's upbringing." — **Chya Barrett**

CHAPTER EIGHT

WHEN THEY MOVE ON

"Last night I lost the world, and gained the universe."
C. JoyBell C

CHAPTER 8

When They Move On

There will come a time, if it hasn't already, when your co-parent will move on from you. They'll start dating. They'll find another "bae." They'll find a new "love of their life." They'll find someone else to give pet names to—and I hate to be the bearer of bad news, but it may be some of the same ones they called you. They'll find someone else to dedicate songs to—and I hate to be the bearer of bad news again, but some of those tracks may be the same ones they dedicated to you. I may or may not be guilty of recycling nicknames and song dedications. I'm going to have to plead the fifth on that one. Anyway, I digress. My point is that at some point, what was once yours will belong to someone else.

The easy part is accepting the reality that you are no longer with the mother or father of your child. The easy part is two people adapting to going from being in a relationship together to both being single. We've all been in relationships before that didn't work out. In time, those romantic feelings you once had for that person usually fade. If we're honest, they could have dissipated long before the two of you officially called it quits.

Here's another familiar scenario—being in a relationship that eventually ends and then having to see our ex hugged up in photos on social media with someone else Whether we want to admit it or not, that might sting. But even though that might bother us a little bit, that's not the real issue. We can get over that.

"WHO THE [CENSORED] IS"

This is where the curve ball is thrown. I want to speak on behalf of the men for a little bit. The real issue is accepting the fact that another man whom we do not know is going to be around our kids. These are the thoughts a man may have to himself, share with his friends, or say to the mother of his children. It's levels to it.

1. "Man, whoever she ends up dating, I just hope he don't bring any street [censored] around my kids."

2. "This new dude she's dating better not start no [censored].

3. "Bro, I don't want to have to beat the [censored] out of her new dude, but I don't play about my kids."

4. "I know her [censored] better not be bringing no [censored] around my kids."

5. "Who the [censored] is this [censored] you got around my kids?"

Now, I'll admit that some of these thoughts can be a bit aggressive. I'm probably guilty of the first three. As a man, having thoughts like 'I wish a [censored] would' regarding our children is normal. As for examples 4 and 5, I've never taken it to that extreme. But then again, I've never felt I had to. Certain situations may require a man to ask, 'Who the [censored] is this [censored] you have around my kids?' depending on the specific individuals the mother has around the children. Let me elaborate on that.

Some women are only attracted to "bad boys" and "street dudes." Some men are only attracted to "ratchet girls" and "crazy chicks." They all exist. Not to toot my horn too much, but I like to consider myself a good dude and a positive individual. When I'm around my son, he gets a positive experience—not perfect, but positive. When my son is around his mother, he receives a positive experience—not perfect, but positive. That's what most of us want for our kids. The negative often gets introduced to our children from sources outside of us. As we all know, It's usually from things outside of our homes. But it can also be from the thing (person) that someone has brought inside the house—the "bad boy," "street dude," "ratchet girl," or "crazy chick." They all exist.

There are men who see no problem bringing drugs, guns, and violence around children. Some will do everything in their power to corrupt these young minds. Certain individuals will subject the mother to verbal and physical abuse in the presence of the children. Regrettably, some [censored] men will inflict physical and sexual harm on innocent children. In essence, some men are just not good people. However, here's the unfortunate reality—some women will expose their children to these 'not good people,' even when they are aware that it's harmful to them.

That's our concern as fathers—that the mother of our child might choose a man we don't approve of to be around our kids. If we know that some guy in the same household as our children meets any of those 'not good people' criteria, we may ask, 'Who the [censored] is this [censored] you got around my kids?' And here's the crazy part: it doesn't even matter if we, too, meet any of those criteria.

Now, what if we don't know? What if we have no evidence that the man being brought around our kids is "not good people?" He could be a solid and good person for all we know. The reaction could be (and should be) to fall back and trust that the mother of our child has made the right decision. On the flip side, because there's still that "I don't know that dude" factor in our mind, the reaction can also be, "Who the [censored] is this [censored] you got around my kids?" That is probably the most challenging part of co-parenting. The uncertainty and lack of control over "Who the [censored] they got around our kids?" That being said, how did I react when I encountered one of these potential "Who the [censored]" situations?

ACCEPTANCE

I trust Tracey's judgment when it comes to the type of men she may introduce to our son. However, that trust doesn't extend to whoever she's dating, nor does it eliminate curiosity. I remember meeting a guy she was dating. I initially learned about him the same way most men do—when a woman mentions her 'friend' in conversation. Typically, when a woman says, 'My friend,' please note that 9.7 times out of 10, that 'friend' is not another woman. Not only that, but there's also a strong likelihood that this 'friend' is more than just a friend. Fellas, you're welcome.

Anyway, one night, we arranged to meet up with each other at a central location so that I could pick up Ahmari. She let me know ahead of time that someone was going to be with her. I presume she did that out of courtesy and respect, and I respect that. She didn't want to surprise me and make it awkward. Here's what my thinking was:

She didn't want me to pull up, and some random dude I'd never heard of before hops out of the same car my son was in, and now I'm standing there with the, "Who the [censored] is this [censored] you got around my kids?" look on my face.

I remember feeling a certain way before meeting the guy. I wasn't sure what that feeling was. Could it be jealousy? Was it anger? Could it be bitterness? Was I not happy for her? Am I a player hater? I had no idea what it was. All I know is that from the moment I realized she was seeing someone, there were times when I would get this feeling. It wasn't until I met the guy, got back in my car, and drove off before I figured out exactly what it was.

When I met him, he got out of the car, we approached each other, and he introduced himself. We had a little small talk for a couple of minutes, and that was that. We got back in our cars and went our separate ways. Instantly, that feeling that I had went away. I could confirm that it wasn't jealousy, anger, or bitterness. The moment I got in the car, I realized that what I was feeling was a weird combination of anticipation, uncertainty, and maybe a little bit of "Who the [censored] is this [censored] she got around my kid?" But after meeting him, I was certain I was happy for her. I felt comfortable with the man she had around my kid.

So what was it? He seemed solid. He was respectful. If I were to judge a book by its cover, I don't think his book contained a lot of violence and explicit content. He appeared to be a good fit for Tracey. He seemed like a positive man my son could be around. Did I truly know him? Of course not. He could have been a mentally unstable drug kingpin for all I knew. But in most cases, all we have to rely on are first impressions, and he made a good one.

That brought me some peace. I also asked Ahmari how he felt about the guy. Plus, of course, I did some detective work and checked him out on social media. Don't act like you never looked someone up. So, I felt comfortable and no longer had that strange mix of anticipation, uncertainty, and the 'Who the [censored] is this [censored] she has around my kid?' feeling. All I needed to do was finally meet the man.

So far in this chapter, I spoke from a man's perspective. Because, of course, I'm a man. But it's not lost on me that women may share a lot of the same feelings. For the women reading this book, relate it to your own situation if it fits. As I said earlier—some men are only attracted to "ratchet girls," and "crazy chicks." Women go through many of the same things men do. I'm sure that when a woman also sees that their co-parent has moved on, they too say to themselves, and their friends—"Who the [censored] is this [censored] HE got around my kid?"

BONUS PARENT

Accepting the addition of another parental figure in your child's life heavily depends on your current involvement in it. If Tracey were to alienate me from my son and keep him away from me, while introducing another man to play a fatherly role to him, I would have strong reservations. First and foremost, I wouldn't accept the situation; I would feel upset with her and might even harbor negative feelings toward this new figure in my son's life. These emotions could stem from the fear of being replaced or losing my son, making me potentially resent this man.

Some of these feelings are understandable, given the circumstances. However, if you're actively fulfilling your role as a parent, and then an additional layer of parental presence is introduced into your child's life, there's more potential upside than downside.

There are these new terms people use today: "bonus parent," "bonus mom," and "bonus dad." It takes a village. In most cases, no one is trying to replace anyone as the father or mother. You know who you are to those children, and you know what you mean to those children. Unless your co-parent has talked bad about you so much to the kids you share, in their eyes, you will always be the #1 man or woman in their life. Embrace change. Respect that added parental figure—that bonus parent if it gets that serious. Respect their relationship. Fellas, invite him over to watch a football game or something. Ladies, go to the nail salon with her.

Listen, It's coo to be coo. It's okay to be cordial. Not only should we not be at war with our co-parents, but we should also not be at war with their new partners. We are all grown-ass men and women. Peace and war do not occupy the same space. If your co-parent has someone else in their lives and they are good and respectable people, don't treat them like an enemy. They may want the same thing you want—for your children to thrive. It should not be an issue as long as they're not stepping on anyone's toes. It takes a village. Again, It's coo to be coo!

A MOTHER'S PERSPECTIVE:
Removing Emotions

"AHHH, when they move on. I won't lie and say this is an easy topic to write about. I think "when they move on" depends on your relationship with your children's father(s). For me, having two co-parents with different situations required me to heal. Straight up. There were levels to it. Although the situations involved different circumstances, there were two facts for both.

1. They would move on to someone else; therefore, co-parenting is the only relationship between us
.
2. They both wanted to be present in their children's lives.

As things shift and children grow, new levels of emotions arise. While learning what required healing within me, I was able to master detachment and let parts of my ego die. There is still a constant struggle of being submissive to certain situations and being "gangsta." HOWEVER, being "gangsta" really only prolongs disagreements. Removing emotions and releasing control was the real game changer. By moving in that way, it allowed for better communication and support.

When we began navigating the concept of having bonus parents, my tendency to overthink was out of control. I believe this overthinking stemmed from a lack of confidence and possibly a bruised ego. I was so critical of myself that I co-created with two different men without a commitment to either of them. It became a constant struggle between focusing on motherhood and asking myself, "Why not me?"

114

However, when I finally arrived at the point of saying, "Thank you for not being me," I gained a new perspective on my co-parents.

A big healing moment was when I understood that co-parenting arrangements will always come with unique perspectives and experiences. The important thing is that we learn to embrace the support systems that can contribute to a child's growth and development. I would like to think my co-parents love themselves enough not to have anyone around our children who would not be of great benefit. This is where trust and removing ego are very important.

It takes a lot of growth to welcome diverse influences from the co-parent. Being open to giving them different exposure, viewpoints, skills, and values, hoping it can be valuable as they navigate through life. Believing it can teach adaptability and the ability to see the world from multiple angles. Trusting while learning from various angles, they receive greater wisdom, empathy, and more effective problem-solving.

Emotions, overthinking, and maybe even a little self-doubt will happen. But the more you grow into yourself, you will see there are more advantages to making it less about you and all about the children. The dynamics of co-parenting are distinct in each of my experiences. With my older three children, I was in a long-term relationship with their father, and there isn't a bonus parent involved in our family structure. Conversely, in Alijah's case, I was never in a relationship with his father, and we co-parent alongside a loving bonus mother. Navigating various co-parenting dynamics has provided me with valuable wisdom and insight into maintaining a solid foundation." —**Chya Barrett**

CHAPTER

NINE

BEFORE IT BREAKS

"Happiness, like unhappiness, is a proactive choice."
Stephen R. Covey

CHAPTER 9

Before It Breaks

Before the "War" begins; before the insults are routine; before the plates are thrown and the cars are keyed; before the exposing on social media; before the papers are filed; before the household is split apart; before the father goes his way and the mother goes her way; before the children only see both parents in each other's presence on exchanges; before the fight over custody and visitation, and before someone finds love elsewhere—there is always that opportunity to hold on to what you have and keep your family intact under one roof before it's too late.

BROKEN PHASE

A relationship has different phases. The beginning is always the most special. We typically go from *attraction* to *interest*, *dating* to *commitment*, and *love* to *marriage* (or long-term relationship). But no matter how blissful it is in the beginning, there are two phases that aren't as enjoyable. All relationships will have ups and downs, but when you start to have more downs than ups, It begins to fall into that *crisis* phase. This is when we encounter an issue with our partner so deep that it causes a crack in the foundation we've built together. When we are unable or unwilling to seal and repair that crack, that is when we enter the *broken phase*. But how do we know if something is genuinely broken if we never tried to repair it?—if we never entered the *repair phase*? Correct me if I'm wrong, but a broken arm will heal.

The first option should always be to fight for what we have built. A non-toxic household held together is better than one split apart. Ideally, a two-parent household is almost always the best option for the children. I say "almost" because not everyone is meant to be together. The reality is that not all romantic relationships are reconcilable. Not every relationship that enters that *broken phase* can be repaired. And because of that, our household can become so toxic that it affects our children. Eventually, after we've exhausted all other options, we may get to a place where we see no other alternative but to give up. Sometimes, the best choice for the children is for their parents to go their separate ways. But we should never lose sight of that first option—to fight.

ACCOUNTABILITY

There are times when I get the question that all divorcees get at some point: Would I get married again? Immediately following my divorce, my answer was a capitalized "HELL NAH!" That's a response that should surprise no one. But over time, I've learned a couple of things that would change my frame of mind in that sense.

1. We shouldn't come to a conclusion like that based on one particular individual during a specific moment in our life that just so happens not to work out.

2. We have that reaction before ever taking ownership and accountability.

We can think of a grandmother's grocery list of reasons why it's the other person's fault, but how often do we look ourselves in the mirror and say, "You [censored] up too." We seldom look at ourselves and question, "What could I have done better or differently? How could I have been a better partner? Did I cause it? Did I worsen it? Yes, they had their issues, but did I trigger any of them? A better question: Could I have saved it? The best question: Did I even attempt to?

We spend so much time and energy blaming the other person that we convince ourselves that we have no responsibility whatsoever in the demise of our relationship. Of course, the blame could primarily be on the other person. It could even solely be on the other person. They could not have treated us the way that we deserved. They could have been horrible human beings. They could have been a lot of things. Not everyone needs to look at themselves in the mirror and ask those questions, but for those that do, try it. I know I did, and I got answers. I'll go first.

What could I have done better or differently? I could have been more affectionate and romantic. I could have talked to her more. I could have traveled with her. I could've not been so damn cheap. I could've refrained from calling her 'crazy.' I could have taken her feelings more seriously. I could have heeded the advice of my best friend, Marcus, and his wife, Ahmiel—when they offered marital advice that might have ultimately saved our marriage if I had listened. I could have believed in our marriage. Most importantly, I could have been there for her when she lost her father. I could've avoided making assumptions. I could have taken responsibility and made necessary adjustments.

Could I have saved it? I know the exact moment when it reached the point of no return. Understanding that moment allows me to gauge how much time I had before that point to mend whatever was broken in our marriage. If I had taken accountability sooner, I believe I could have saved our marriage. In fact, if I had made specific adjustments earlier, I don't think our marriage would have ever reached a point where it needed saving.

Did I make an attempt to (save our marriage)? First, I'm not suggesting that by merely 'doing better,' 'being a better husband,' and attempting to 'save' our marriage, we would still be together today. I could have transformed into the type of person only seen in movies, and we might have still ended up in this same co-parenting situation a year later. However, we will never know if we can make a shot we never take. There was no genuine effort on my part to save my marriage. I didn't sit down with her and attempt to work through our issues. I didn't seek any guidance or marriage counseling. Also, back then, there weren't as many of these self-proclaimed relationship gurus online as we have today, so I didn't have them to turn to either. All I had, like many of us, were resources and people around us that we failed to tap into because we never took accountability first.

So I'm clear, these are not questions that should only be asked after the fact—when the household is split apart. These are questions that should be asked before or when it gets to that crisis phase. Being preventative while you're in your relationship is better than being reactive after it ends. No one wants to be in a "shoulda, woulda, coulda" situation if they could avoid it.

Instead of

~~"What could I have done better?"~~
"What can I do better?"
"I will become better."

~~"Could I have saved my relationship?"~~
"How can I save my relationship?"
"What can I do to where we don't even get to that point?"

~~"Did I attempt to save it?"~~
"What can I do to save it?"
"I'm doing everything in my power right now."

Not all relationships can or should be saved, but it's always worth it to try—especially when there are little ones involved. Fight for what you once had. Don't take your partner for granted. Never think they won't reach a boiling point. Be respectful. Be faithful. Be transparent. Be private, but seek guidance from those you trust and whose opinions you value. Have discernment. Listen to how they feel, not only what they say. Keep your personal business off social media. Be considerate, fair, and willing to compromise. Communicate, comprehend, and have an understanding of your significant other. Support them at all times. Show them they're appreciated. Ask questions. Get to know them more and more each day. And lastly, maintain peace in your relationship.

CHAPTER TEN

FINAL THOUGHTS

"Love is an endless act of forgiveness.
Forgiveness is the key to action and freedom."
Nikki Giovanni, Poet

CHAPTER 10
Final Thoughts

Imagine doing something stressful every day for an extended period of time. Experiences like these can cause an immense amount of stress, anxiety, or anger. If you've ever worked a job you hated, imagine that. Have you ever been in a place where you were constantly looking at a clock waiting for the time to be up? In those situations, does time seem to move faster or slower? I'm going to assume that it's slower, and those are the times you may say something like, "This is taking forever." When that happens, does that experience then become more or less enjoyable?

EIGHTEEN YEARS

That is the feeling that many parents have had for eighteen years. That's the age at which a child will then be considered an adult. Eighteen years is a long time. Eighteen years of co-parenting shouldn't feel like a prison sentence, where we are counting down the days for it to be up. That makes it feel like "forever." So many parents are in survival mode—just trying to get through the eighteen years so that they no longer have to deal with the stress, anxiety, and anger that may come with their co-parent.

Eighteen years of raising children should be the most blissful years of our lives, not the most stressful. That's a long time as it is, but it feels even longer when we are suffering through it simultaneously.

ASK YOURSELF

Whether I am the warden or the inmate, do I want eighteen years of raising children to feel like a prison sentence?

How can I be a better co-parent?

How can I be a better parent?

Is it me?

Was I wrong?

How can I be a better person?

Are we truly doing what's in the best interest of the child?

What would I want if I were in my child's shoes?

Do I want to live a life devoid of toxicity?

What do I need to apologize for?

If they are deserving, how can I show my appreciation to them?

How can we collaborate more?

Do I need to get better at communicating?

ASK YOURSELF

Are they always being disrespectful, or am I just sometimes not comprehending what they're saying?

Should I compromise more? How would I feel if I had no control?

Am I being fair?

What have I not forgiven them for?

Am I reliable? Can I be counted on?

In what ways can I support my co-parent?

Are there times that I can be more understanding?

Do I want peace?

CHANGE THE NARRATIVE

Everyone who gets married will not be together forever. There will always be children raised in two-parent households and children raised in two households with a parent in each. There will always be relationships that will one day come to an end. There will always be children raised in single-parent households with one parent completely absent. However, that outcome should not be normalized. Two people not working out romantically should never be the reason our children are not raised by both parents in non-toxic environments. Co-parent so well that they don't know the difference.

CHANGE THE NARRATIVE

I don't claim to have the perfect example of a co-parenting relationship, although it's a strong one. There are areas that could use some improvement. I don't aim to be the "expert" with all the right answers. I don't consider myself an "expert" or an authority on relationships of any kind. That title doesn't move me. However, I am an expert when it comes to sharing my own experiences, and what I know has worked for me.

Here's what I also know: I know that I'm tired of witnessing and hearing about my people treating the other parent of their child poorly for reasons that not even a genius psychologist with a 200 IQ could make sense of. We have to think more about the children. We must do better. Let us all have healthy co-parenting relationships with the absence of toxicity. Let's not be at war. Let's change the narrative.

Respect & Gratitude!

RESOURCES & INFORMATION

THE CUSTODY PLANS

Here are 7 different parenting time schedules where each parent has the child(ren) 50% of the time. Feel free to make adjustments if needed so it fits with your specific situation. (Source: Custodyxchange.com)

1. **Alternating Weeks:** 1 week with one parent and the next week with the other.

2. **2 Weeks Each:** 2 weeks with one parent and 2 weeks with the other.

3. **3-4-4-3 Schedule:** 3 days with one parent, 4 days with the other. Then, switch. 4 days with the first parent, 3 days with the other.

4. **2-2-5-5 Schedule:** 2 days with each parent and then 5 days with each parent.

5. **2-2-3 Schedule:** 2 days with one parent, 2 days with the other parent, and 3 days with the first parent. Switch the following week.

6. **Alternating 2 Days:** Switch between each parent every 2 days.

7. **Alternate Each Day & Weekend:** Switch between each parent every day and alternate weekends.

THE MEANINGS

Always keep these definitions in mind!

Apology: a regretful acknowledgment of an offense or failure (admitting when you're wrong).

Appreciation: Recognition and enjoyment of the good qualities of someone or something.

Collaboration: The action of working with someone to produce or create something.

Communication: The exchange of ideas and thoughts between two or more individuals.

Comprehension: The action or capability of understanding something.

Compromise: An agreement or a settlement of a dispute that is reached by each side making concessions.

THE MEANINGS

Considerate: Careful not to cause inconvenience or hurt others.

Fair: Without cheating or trying to achieve an unjust advantage.

Forgiveness: Stop feeling angry or resentful toward someone for (an offense, flaw, or mistake).

Support: To give assistance, approval, comfort, or encouragement.

Reliable: Consistently good in quality or performance; able to be trusted.

Understanding: The ability to learn, judge, and make decisions.

Family: YOU and your co-parent.

JVION JONES

Website

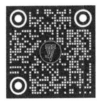

www.JvionVision.com

Email: info@jvionvision.com

Social Media
Instagram: @jvionvision
Instagram: @TheGiftofExperiencePodcast
Facebook: Jvion Vision
YouTube: @TheGiftofExperiencePodcast

ABOUT THE AUTHOR

Jvion Jones is a father, author, speaker, mentor, and entrepreneur hailing from Northern California. As an author, Jvion Jones has penned seven compelling books that explore a wide range of subjects, showcasing his versatility as a writer. Beyond his literary pursuits, he is deeply committed to mentoring, coaching, and uplifting the youth—sharing his wisdom and experiences to inspire the next generation. In addition to his literary and mentoring endeavors, Jvion is an entrepreneur who owns an apparel printing company, combining his creative flair with business acumen.

In 2021, Jvion's life took an unexpected turn when he was diagnosed with glioblastoma brain cancer. This formidable battle has not deterred his indomitable spirit; rather, it has fueled his desire to make a lasting impact on the world through his words. His dedication to his craft, mentorship, and entrepreneurship exemplifies his unwavering commitment to leaving a lasting legacy. Jvion continues to shine brightly in both the literary and music worlds.

CHYA BARRETT

Website

www.livingwithnoapologies.com

Email: info@livingwithnoapologies.com

Social Media

Instagram: @livingwithnoapologies

Facebook: Living With No Apologies

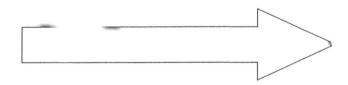

ABOUT THE AUTHOR

"Hi, my name is **Chya Barrett**, pronounced CH-ii-YA. I am the founder and CEO of No Apologies, LLC, an empowerment organization created to uplift, support, and encourage individuals to walk in their truth unapologetically. #NoApologies holds a unique meaning for each person I encounter, as each individual comes from diverse backgrounds and has different life experiences. I've always known that my life was far from ordinary. However, it was through trials, followed by years of therapy, soul-searching, and personal development, that I was able to uncover the root of who I am and what I have to offer the world.

Creation, Co-Inspiration, and Connection are the core principles that underpin the #NoApologies mission. I hold these ideals close to my heart and cultivate them daily, as I continuously connect with new sources of inspiration. Today, as I confidently stand in my divine feminine power, I can look in my rearview mirror and understand that each 'life pivot' was purposeful and necessary. Through #NoApologies, it is my deepest desire to use this platform to inspire individuals to explore their truths and discover what it means for them to LIVE with #NoApologies."

OTHER BOOKS BY Jvion

References

"50/50 Custody & Visitation Schedules: 7 Examples." Custody Exchange, www.custodyxchange.com/topics/schedules/50-50/7-examples.php.

Leon, J. (2017, October 17). *Don't Call Her 'Baby Mama.'* Level.Medium. https://level.medium.com/please-dont-call-her-my-baby-mama-bf8be35d151c

Wikipedia, en.wikipedia.org/wiki/Negotiation.

Elliot, B. (2017, October 17). *Historical Marriage Trends from 1890-2010: A Focus on Race Differences.* chrome-extension://efaidnbmnnnibpcajpcglclefindmkaj/https://www.census.gov/content/dam/Census/library/working-papers/2012/demo/SEHSD-WP2012-12.pdf

(n.d.). *4 Problems With The Modern Child Support System.* Dads Divorce. https://dadsdivorce.com/articles/4-problems-with-the-modern-child-support-system/

"DIVORCE STATISTICS: OVER 115 STUDIES, FACTS AND RATES FOR 2022." WF Lawyers, www.wf-lawyers.com/divorce-statistics-andfacts/#:~:text=Almost%2050%20percent%20of%20all,first%20marriages%20end%20in%20divorce.

Quotes Index

Made in the USA
Las Vegas, NV
26 November 2023

81076658R80090